M000209199

ADVANCE PRAISE

"Kyle & Gary do a fantastic job of laying out the things involved with apartment investing that many are just not educated on and not enough people are talking about. Reading this book will separate you from your competition when executing your business plan while growing wealth for you and your investors."

—NEAL BAWA, FOUNDER AND CEO, GROCAPITUS

*"I see many people get into commercial real estate and think, 'If I can only find the opportunities and raise the money, I can do deals!' Those are extremely important aspects to **building** your real estate portfolio...but Asset Management is critical to **keeping** your real estate portfolio. The work doesn't end once you close on a property; that's when the work really begins. You've gotta have your ducks in a row, and Kyle & Gary give you the tools to do exactly that in this book. Their insights are profound; don't take them lightly!"*

—TIM BRATZ, CEO, LEGACY WEALTH HOLDINGS, @TIMBRATZ

"Asset management isn't the sexiest part of the real estate sector, but it is the key difference maker between those who will only succeed when the market is favorable and those who will protect and grow investors' capital through all stages of the economic cycle. Gary & Kyle have provided a ton of great content about best practices in asset management through their podcast and summit, and this book puts it all in one easily accessible place."

—HUNTER THOMPSON, AUTHOR OF
RAISING CAPITAL FOR REAL ESTATE

"Gary & Kyle share a ton of best practices to help you become a better operator. This book is a great road map for beginner to intermediate operators looking to gain a competitive advantage in a tight market. Who doesn't want to learn ways to increase their NOI?"

—BRANDON HALL, CEO, HALL CPA PLLC

"If you want to learn how to be a successful Asset Manager, then read this book. Gary & Kyle go over many of the scenarios that an operator will face. It doesn't matter if you manage a couple of units or many thousands; this book will help guide you to be better."

—GENE TROWBRIDGE, FOUNDING PARTNER,
TROWBRIDGE LAW GROUP LLP

"As a passive and active multifamily investor, I frequently reference this book for the invaluable asset management systems and strategies. The outlined principles have boosted my confidence to be able to manage any size deal. Gary & Kyle have truly inspired me to become a Best in Class multifamily operator!"

—ROBBY WOO, CO-FOUNDER, TRWOO INVESTMENTS LLC

HOW TO MANAGE YOUR
MULTIFAMILY ASSET, AVOID MISTAKES, AND
BUILD WEALTH THROUGH REAL ESTATE

BEST
IN
CLASS

KYLE
MITCHELL

GARY
LIPSKY

ASSET MANAGEMENT MASTERY
PUBLISHING

COPYRIGHT © 2021 KYLE MITCHELL & GARY LIPSKY

All rights reserved.

BEST IN CLASS

*How to Manage Your Multifamily Asset, Avoid
Mistakes, and Build Wealth through Real Estate*

ISBN   978-1-5445-2089-6 *Paperback*
         978-1-5445-2088-9 *Ebook*

To my amazing daughters, Arielle and Jadyn, whom I strive to show that you can do anything you set your mind to. This book was a lot harder to write than I thought it would be, and they kept me motivated to write and finish the best book possible. To my parents, who have always been incredibly supportive and are two of my biggest cheerleaders. They helped shape the person I've become today, and I am very grateful for that. And to my brother, David, and sister, Laurie, who are always there for me; it means the world to me.

—Gary

To the love of my life, Lalita. If it were not for you, I would likely still only be hoping that one day I will pursue my dreams. But instead, your love, support, and true partnership helped push me out of my comfort zones and into a life we both visualized and have now made a reality. You are my rock. I also want to thank my forever loving and supportive parents, who believed I would be great in anything I set out to achieve. They never questioned my dreams, which instilled a confidence in me to make those dreams my reality.

—Kyle

CONTENTS

BOOK ACKNOWLEDGMENTS

We couldn't have written this book without all the lessons we learned from so many others. From our amazing guests on our *Asset Management Mastery Podcast* to the countless conferences we have attended and even hosted, podcasts we listened to, and books we read that gave us the knowledge necessary to write it all down in one place.

Special thanks to Sarafina Riskind and the team at Scribe for guiding us through the process of writing this book.

FOREWORD

BY JOE FAIRLESS, AUTHOR OF *BEST EVER APARTMENT SYNDICATION BOOK* AND CO-FOUNDER OF ASHCROFT CAPITAL

What do the following scenarios have in common?

- Taking a charge to create a turnover in basketball
- Bunting a runner over to a scoring position in baseball
- A running back blocking a blitzing linebacker to give the quarterback time to throw

Yes, they are all sports-related situations. But let's dig deeper. What do each of these situations have in common?

None are sexy, but all are necessary for the team to accomplish a winning outcome.

For example, when is the last time you heard the following?

"Oh man, what a game. Did you see that clutch BUNT that Jerome pulled off? Dang, what a stud!"

Or, "I can't wait to go see the Lakers play tonight. Oh no, I'm not going to see LeBron play. I just want to see them draw some CHARGES on defense! That's the stuff of legends."

Or even, "Why are you talking about that one-handed catch? Didn't you see the TECHNIQUE of the running back picking up the blitz? Picture perfect!"

It's silly because it just doesn't happen. But it should because anyone who has been on a team knows there are roles and responsibilities that are undervalued *and* necessary for achieving successful outcomes. And that's why this book is so important.

This book goes deep into an aspect of owning apartments that many don't focus on and generally isn't talked about enough. The sexy parts of multifamily investing tend to be raising money and finding the deal. Listen to a podcast or just speak to others at a meetup and you'll hear the conversation slant toward how investors raised their money or secured their deal.

I think this focus is prevalent because raising money and

finding a deal have to do with the acquisitions part of the process, and we tend to gain fulfillment through creating things as opposed to maintaining them. I'd certainly (successfully) argue asset management isn't maintenance but rather creation, but unfortunately, I believe a lot of multifamily real estate investors, especially beginners, look at asset management as maintenance. As this book outlines, that is far from the reality. Asset management requires the same level of creative ingenuity that finding a deal does. And it likely has even more unexpected twists and turns than anything that happens before you close the deal (as you'll read more about in the Curveballs chapter).

So, bravo to you for being in the minority of people who can appreciate and understand the value of asset management. You are here to learn how these necessary skills will help you be a successful multifamily owner. One of the greatest risks associated with any deal is in the execution of the business plan, and you are taking proactive steps to mitigate that risk for you and your investors.

INTRODUCTION

When you learn, teach. When you get, give.

—MAYA ANGELOU

Say you've closed your first real estate deal as Asset Manager. This is a big deal for you—you've worked hard to get here. You've read the books that teach you about how to get started, how to raise capital, how to close—and you've done it! You have your first property! Congratulations.

But a few months down the line, things aren't quite going according to plan. Nothing is on schedule, you're not sure how to hold people accountable, and now, the despair is mounting. How will you get this property turned around on time? Will you get the rents you forecasted? How do you get your third-party property management team to listen to you?

This book is here to help. It is a guide on how to become a Best in Class operator. It was written for all those starting out on their journeys as operators and Asset Managers who don't know what it takes to run this business and feel lost and unsure of where to turn. If that's you—welcome! Of course, if you've been in this business a while and haven't been seeing the results you want, this book is for you too. There are a lot of real estate coaches and programs on the market that help you get your first property but very few that address what happens after you actually acquire a property. And that's a shame. Proper asset management is critical to your investment success: it will not only put more money in your pocket now but will help you grow exponentially over time.

Perhaps you could get away with poor asset management from 2010 to 2019, when real estate values kept going up and up. But it's when the market tightens—when there's a natural disaster or you find yourself staring at a black swan event like COVID-19—that the good Asset Managers really separate themselves from the not so good. That's when consistent, upper-tier asset management makes all the difference. Many good properties have suffered from bad asset management. People get lazy, lack consistency, or trust too much in their property management team to monitor them and ensure the job actually gets done and gets done right. Conversely, we have seen bad properties perform well because of *good* asset management. These operators solve problems, hold everyone accountable, measure everything, and are consistent. Good asset management is not a hobby—it is a job, a passion! And no matter how lost you've felt or how badly you've failed before, you can learn to be better at it.

Here's where we come in. We believe that good asset management is not rocket science. You have to be consistent. You have to pay attention to the details. You have to implement systems and processes to identify bottlenecks and not be afraid to ask a lot of questions. Mistakes happen, but they can be fixed if you pay attention. The devil is in the details: we have seen far too many operators not pay attention to the details, and their investors have suffered. *They* have suffered.

That is why we wrote this book. It's a practical, in-depth guide to what it takes to become a Best in Class operator. It teaches you what details you need to pay attention to. We've interviewed over 150 successful operators to get their expertise on everything—from leasing to driving income to reducing expenses, all of it is in this book. Chapters are divided according to topic, so you can flip back to the relevant chapter at any time and refresh your memory on what it takes to perfect that task. We've tried not to include too many minute details—we don't want to bore you—but everything you need to know about how to be a highly effective Asset Manager is in these pages.

Ultimately, our goal is to get you to a place where you feel confident with your capabilities as an Asset Manager— where you don't feel lost or confused. We want you to be on the path to growth. We have a combined experience of half a century in business management and operations, and we've learned the best way to grow is to learn from other people's mistakes. This is your chance to learn from ours and from all the successful operators we've interviewed over the years. Here's a bit more about us, in detail:

We met up at a real estate conference a few years ago. We had networked with each other a few times in the past and knew we were both scheduled to look at properties in the same markets in the near future. We eventually decided to tour properties in Arizona together. Over many long days, we realized our values, work ethics, and goals were similar, and we decided to continue to work together through our separate companies. After partnering on two deals under our independent company names, we decided it was more effective and efficient to form one company, not only for us but for our investors as well.

We decided to name the company APT Capital Group. APT stands for Alignment, Prosperity, and Transparency, which are the values we want to incorporate into everything our company does. We knew with our combined fifty-plus years of business and operational experience, asset management was going to be our superpower. All our prior experiences helped create who we are today, and we leverage those experiences to be Best in Class.

GARY LIPSKY

I became an entrepreneur at a young age. I grew up in New Jersey, and as a teenager, I ran an auto detailing business during the warm months and a snow shoveling business in the winter. In college, I started a restaurant delivery service many years before DoorDash, Grubhub, or Postmates existed, and I co-produced a few independent films in my twenties. I learned early on that whatever work I put in, I'd be rewarded for it eventually. If I was not out hustling for my business, thinking about my business, or nurturing it, it would not grow. I had the hustle part down early on, but I needed to learn how to take advantage of other people's experiences to provide rocket fuel for my own business.

Some of my professional highlights are as follows:

- Started investing in value-add real estate in 2002.
- Founded arc, an afterschool-programs, outdoor-education, and leadership-development company, and ran it for sixteen years. Arc grew to over 700 employees, including growth during the Great Recession, and worked with 9,000 students every day. I sold arc at the end of 2016 to go into real estate full time.
- Started a nonprofit, CORE Educational Services, in

2006, which works with at-risk youth in Southern California.

- Invested passively in 1,500 units before syndicating my first property.
- Succeeded in becoming a lead sponsor and Asset Manager on hundreds of units worth over tens of millions of dollars.

Selling arc was one of the hardest things I've ever had to do, but I got the bug for real estate when I purchased my first single-family home in 2002. It was scary and exciting at the same time, but I knew this was just the beginning. I loved how I could use my creative side to instantly figure out how to add more value to a property. I also loved being able to look at the numbers and see if the business plan made sense. Once a solid business plan was put in place, it was a thrill to implement it and see it come to fruition. I knew real estate was my true calling and wanted to devote all my time to becoming the best real estate investor and Asset Manager I could be.

I became certified in Real Estate Financial Modeling and listened to podcasts, read books, and attended conferences and meetups to educate myself. I invested in other people's deals before taking on my own so I could learn what others were doing right and what they were doing wrong. All these experiences taught me a lot, and I use them to help guide me today. Real estate is a team sport. You can theoretically do it on your own, but you will probably be more successful, and it will be easier, working with others. Join a mastermind group, get a mentor, or learn from others. It will help you get to where you want to go much faster.

KYLE MITCHELL

Nothing great comes easy! I have had hands-on experience of that fact. I vividly remember the details of what I had to do to get my first property. It wasn't easy and wouldn't have been possible without Lalita, my wife. We haven't looked back since that first successful property.

Every month, Lalita and I would drive eight hours to Tucson, Arizona, at 2:00 a.m. on our only day off from our full-time, W-2 jobs. Once in Tucson, we would spend hours touring properties and meeting with brokers and local investors. There were times when we would not get back home until 1:00 a.m. the following day. We did this once a month for about eight months.

On one of these drives, a broker I had been building a relationship with over the past five or six months called us and said he had a property he literally just received the keys to, and he invited us and our property management company to tour it with him. Because we were in the right place at the right time, we had a three-week head start before this property went to market, and we were able to lock it down pretty quickly thereafter. Hard work, persistence, and relationships were the keys to us getting our first deal. If you do things others are not willing to do, you will find yourself achieving more than others can ever hope to.

I have been in management and operations since 2003 and investing in real estate since 2010. In my time as a regional manager, I have learned the importance of building the right team and implementing systems and procedures to streamline and drive my businesses while utilizing these systems to hold all parties accountable. I have developed an eye for seeing and analyzing details clearly (through this book, you will learn how to do this as well). Attention to detail, consistency, and communicating with 100 percent transparency have been major keys to my success. True success also lies in the details and follow up, and these are two things you will learn throughout this book.

Some of my professional highlights are as follows:

- Played golf at a professional level.
- Hired by American Golf as the youngest general manager, at the time, at the age of twenty-one.
- Acted as point person for the 2014 National Championship and Rose Bowl Alumni Tailgates, serving almost 40,000 guests, managing over 900 employees, and generating more than $2.6 million in revenue in two days.

- Worked in property management for golf courses for twenty-plus years while managing over 250 employees and $20 million in revenue on a day-to-day basis.
- Turned American Golf's mismanaged and worst-performing golf courses into high-performing golf courses.
- Succeeded in becoming a lead sponsor and Asset Manager on hundreds of units worth over tens of millions of dollars.

My passion is helping others reach their goals in all areas of life by doing things the right way and creating long-lasting relationships based on trust and clarity. I hope this book can be one of the stepping stones along my journey to helping you reach your goals.

* * *

Asset management is critical to your real estate business, and every small step you take toward being a Best in Class operator will not only help you grow your net worth but help others as well. This book aims to fill the education gap when it comes to asset management, and we believe it will be invaluable to your real estate journey.

Ready? Let's begin!

—Gary and Kyle

CHAPTER 1

ASSET MANAGEMENT

GETTING STARTED

Management is, above all, a practice where art, science, and craft meet.

—HENRY MINTZBERG

Asset management is an ongoing process that involves meticulous attention to detail, information tracking, comprehensive planning, a keen eye on ongoing trends, and the ability to see into the future to make better decisions.

Throughout this book, we'll show you how to maximize the value and return on investment of a property. We will dive into mitigating risks, being proactive, consistently measuring key performance indicators (KPIs), reducing expenditures whenever possible, getting the best out of your team, adding new streams of revenue, maximizing your current streams, and developing strong communication skills.

Being in operations and management for a combined fifty-plus years, we have witnessed many peaks and valleys. Asset management is not the sexiest side of real estate, but it is the most critical. People talk about the size of the deal, how many units, the cost, etc. They do not talk about the actual management of the asset. It is hard work to get a deal, but the work does not end there. The next steps involve capitalizing on the investment.

Many people do not give asset management the focus it needs because they work alone or on a limited scale, and we suggest they reconsider their approach. We are great advocates of collaboration and working with others because you cannot be an expert in everything. Instead, you should rely on your team to break out responsibilities. Even if you work alone, make technology your partner and it will become easier to manage your assets and prosper exponentially. The use of technology—or, as we like to call them, tools—is so important we reserved a full chapter for it at the end of this book.

Asset management is necessary to get the maximum value out of a property. The core purpose of buying real estate is to make money, and if you do not manage assets properly, how can you make money from your investment? You will either not make any money, or you will miss opportunities to get the best returns on your investment. You could potentially get by at 80 to 90 percent effort for a good property during good times, but a little more effort could yield huge profits during good times and survival during bad times.

We picked the order of this book based on a typical asset management journey and the specific topics because we felt these were the most important. It starts with a team, as you can't do it all by yourself. Therefore, we'll discuss how to build a team, both internally and externally, and what to look for in your critical positions.

We'll share best practices in due diligence. This happens before you take over a property, but we felt it was necessary to discuss in this book as it sets you up for success once you close on your purchase. We'll get into budgeting from a 10,000-foot level, including capex and reserves. This is definitely an area where people make a lot of mistakes, and we want to make sure you don't make the same ones. We'll also discuss financial analysis, which is one of the least talked about subjects out there but is also extremely critical. Very few people get their hands dirty delving into their reports, and this is where you will inevitably find mistakes.

Next, we'll get into legal matters. There are a lot of people in the industry doing things wrong. Just because others may have more experience than you doesn't mean they are playing by the rules. Make sure you read Chapter 6 carefully so you stay out of hot water or, even worse, jail.

Some investors think once they close the deal, they can hire a property management company and it's all smooth sailing into a great future. In many cases, these investors are onto the next deal after a couple months; then, they rinse and repeat. To most people, the definition of asset management is very limited in terms of its operations and responsibilities. They rely on a third-party property management team that often manages several to hundreds, if not more, properties. This is not to say they do not work hard, but no one will give your property the singular focus you can. To maximize profit, you cannot afford to overlook this.

You have to be diligent with your asset management, and that requires having KPIs that measure important aspects in order to guide improvements and pinpoint bottlenecks. How do you know what to improve if you are not measuring important metrics?

We'll cover effective ways to market your available units and how best to track leasing. If your units aren't being rented, you are going to struggle to stay afloat. But if you can be an expert in those areas, you are going to be really driving income.

We'll show you how to manage renovations and some of

the best ways to implement a value-add strategy. There are very few properties that don't require work, and some of the best opportunities are ones that need a lot of work. After reading these chapters, you'll know how to avoid pitfalls and make sure things are getting done in a timely fashion that maximizes your investment.

We will also cover how to properly communicate with your investors and deal with curveballs. We assume you'll have investors because at some point, you'll run out of your own money and need to leverage others. You'll also have to deal with the unknown, whether it be weather, a black swan event, or something else. It's impossible to predict everything that will happen, and you'll need to be able to take a punch, get back on your feet quickly, and deal with the situation.

At the time of the writing of this book, COVID-19 lingers on, so there may be many properties available in the near future at discounted prices due to a lack of good asset management. Things can change on a dime, as we have seen with COVID-19, so you can't be asleep at the wheel.

Of course, a book about asset management wouldn't be complete without discussing a topic a lot of people talk about but few understand well: taxes. We are not accountants, but we'll help guide you and provide knowledge about a K-1, which is the form your investors will get for their taxes, assuming you have investors. We'll also show you how to prepare for disposition, things to look out for, and proper planning. Hopefully, you will sell your property for a huge profit one day because you were a diligent Asset Manager!

Another important aspect of asset management is the efficient use of tools. Asset management is a constant process, and you must have eyes on a property on a daily or weekly basis, depending on circumstances. This can be difficult to accomplish. You can partly rely on your team, but you also need to harness the power of time-tested tools to paint the picture of how well you are doing. Indeed, these tools can help facilitate your team and aid them in doing their jobs better. Over the years, we have tested many tools, and we found a few tools to be highly effective in aiding our asset management processes. These include a customer relationship management (CRM) tool, an investor portal, team collaboration and project management tools, and market analysis and business intelligence tools that create our KPIs. We will talk about each tool in detail at the end of this book.

There are also skillsets you need to have to be a successful Asset Manager. Attention to detail, being proactive, and following trends are absolutely necessary if you want to excel as an Asset Manager.

When you do not pay attention to details, you risk costly

mistakes and losses. Being proactive is a demand of today's fast-paced work environment. When you can make informed decisions, you can better stay on top of the game. By employing the following strategic planning and organizational techniques, you are on your way to becoming a proactive Asset Manager:

- Make a comprehensive work plan to outline key functions
- Prepare lists to manage multiple things you need to accomplish and include references of timeframe or deadlines
- Plan in advance for short-term and long-term projects
- Maintain your schedule
- Ask for clarity when you do not understand something

If you are a proactive Asset Manager, you will face fewer problems overall; in fact, you will be able to solve issues before they can become problems. Your proactive attitude will also trickle down to your team over time. Hopefully, many issues will be resolved at the team level, and you will just be informed during reporting. The ultimate benefit will be reflected in your net operating income (NOI) and swelling bank account (i.e., more profit for you and your investors).

Do not be a reactive Asset Manager who waits for problems to occur to address issues, as it usually is too late at that point to resolve the issue. The worst part is reactive people do not have a vision or objectives to follow. They allow problems to pile up, and suddenly, they have an onslaught of problems to deal with—issues they should have been able to avoid or at least predict. We have seen properties go into bankruptcy due to a reactive attitude. The owners did not really have an Asset Manager in place, so they paid no attention at all until it was too late. Their expenses grew, leading to losses, and they ran out of capital reserves to the point they could not do anything about it except do a capital call. We understand this can happen to even the best operators due to extenuating circumstances, but what we're trying to convey is that someone needs to be in charge of the asset and managing it on a consistent basis.

Keeping up to date on the latest trends is also critical and will allow you to forecast the future to some extent. Some of our sources for forecasting real estate trends include CoStar, Yardi, Real Page, and broker reports, and you can get all these reports for free. External factors influence the process as well—for instance, tenant/landlord laws, the economy, and epidemics or pandemics like COVID-19. You need to understand where things are headed and have disaster plans in place. As for local variables, you must know what amenities residents demand, crime rates, new developments, household incomes, population growth, and other trends. Over time, these things can make or break your investment.

Reviewing trends has always helped us stay ahead of the game. For example, one of our purchases was in an area we knew was headed in the right direction. It was in a C class neighborhood, but it was moving toward B class because the median household income was increasing, there was a massive construction project set to begin close by, and schools were being built. These were great trends that would hopefully have a huge effect on our eventual sale and get us greater return on investment. Soon after we purchased the property, an apartment building down the street sold for a significant amount more than what we paid. It was a nicer property, but that was a great comp to show we were correct in our analysis.

On another occasion, a well-regarded charter school was built practically across the street from our property, which is a great draw for future residents. We knew crime was trending down, and residents in local neighborhoods were getting priced out of their current communities. They started to flock to the neighborhood that our apartment building was in and became our residents.

It is important an Asset Manager takes the lead on all things regarding the property. The other sponsors can be on the calls and have access to the reports, but all the info should flow through the Asset Manager so there is a clean line of communication. The Asset Manager should report to the team and provide the necessary information to share with investors.

Assuming you have navigated your property through all the facets of asset management properly, you will eventually bring your property to market and sell it at a hefty profit. The value you added will be proof of your asset management abilities. We hope this book adds many more tools to your toolbox.

Asset management takes a lot of work. Attention to detail, consistency, communication, and following a plan yield great returns. Asset management is not something you should take lightly; since you're reading this book, it's obvious you do not. We wish we had found a book that covered all these topics before we got started. We're glad you found this one.

Let's dive into more detail!

CHAPTER 2

BUILDING A TEAM

Alone we can do so little; together we can do so much.

—HELEN KELLER

The first thing you need to do to become a successful Asset Manager is build a team. It is impossible for you to do everything on your own *and* be an expert on all those things. Even if you are not interested in scaling, you need to rely on others, either within your organization or outside of it, to do the job. Building a team helped one of our friends, Tim Bratz, triple his income and put him on a path to acquire the 4,000-plus doors he owns today. Hiring an assistant freed up his time and allowed him to focus on his strengths. Does tripling your income sound good to you?

Building a team does not happen overnight. It takes many months and even years of developing strong relationships, building trust, and cultivating good communication. In this chapter, we'll explore the components of a good team, both internally and externally; how to hire effectively; best management practices; and much more.

COMPONENTS OF A GOOD TEAM

Putting an internal team in place can be a daunting task, and when I say "internal," I mean specifically those that work for your company. Who do you hire? What roles need to be filled immediately? How do you decide?

The answers to these questions depend largely on you. There is no "definitive must" first hire. Instead, you must create your team based on your strengths and weaknesses. When you start to build your team, list all the things you are best at and where you need the most help. Then select the roles that compensate for your failings, and hire accordingly. If you focus on your strengths and hire for your weaknesses, your company will grow tenfold.

Be honest with yourself when creating this list. This is not something you can create rapid-fire, unless you really know yourself. Take your time, and be thorough. No one can excel at everything—that is why it is always a good idea to surround yourself with people smarter than you. Are you an introvert who prefers sitting behind a desk and doing analysis? Or do you like shaking hands and talking to people over coffee? Are you an idea person or an implementor?

Also think in terms of the highest and best uses of your time. What use of your time creates the biggest impact on your business? What are the key revenue generators? That's where you want your focus to be. It is hard to concentrate and excel when you have too many things on your plate. Trust us, we have tried—and we are still pushing ourselves to outsource more. Your productivity will skyrocket when you can focus on a few things you do well and outsource the rest to your team.

You should also hire for where you are going, not where you are today. Wayne Gretzky has said he would skate to where the puck was going, not where it is. The same is true for business. What got you here will not get you where you are going. So think big. Where do you want your business to go? What skillsets will help you accomplish your goals? Look for a team that can make your vision a reality.

RIGHT PEOPLE IN THE RIGHT SEATS

In asset management, it is important to be intentional with everything you do—and that includes who you hire. Do you want to build a world-class organization? That does not happen without a lot of thought. A bad hire can really set you back, while a great hire can provide rocket fuel for your business. It's important to get it right.

A crucial part of hiring correctly is choosing the right people for the right seats. What we mean by this is you do not want a creative type handling your accounting or an analytic type in charge of communications. Some companies like to test potential employees to see where they'd be a good fit, and we definitely recommend it. It does not cost a lot of money, and it can save you a ton down the road. There are many assessment tools out there, and I suggest you give them a try for yourself. Below are two of the most well-known tools:

1. Myers-Briggs

The Myers-Briggs Type Indicator consists of ninety-three forced-choice questions, where the participant matches a word with a statement. The results from the questionnaire place the person into one of sixteen personalities, each with their own strengths and weaknesses.

2. DISC

DISC is a behavior-assessment non-judgmental tool used to discuss people's behavioral differences. The four personality types are D (dominance), I (influence), S (steadiness), and C (conscientiousness).

The D type cares about performance; they want to break records. Sales and acquisitions are typically good roles for a D. I is more of an interpersonal type; they are typically good in sales. Then you have your Ss, who are more social and supportive. An S would be a good fit for a project manager role. C types are detail oriented and logical. They'd probably be best as your attorney or accountant.

For example, in one of Gary's assessments, he was found to be a Do It Now person followed by Get It Right, In a Caring Way, and, lastly, Make It Fun. These are attributes of a CEO or business owner, which aptly fit his role. He wants to get the work done and is not focused on making it fun. He believes that enjoying what you do is important, and there are times to have fun, but on a day-to-day basis, his assessment indicates an emphasis on getting the work done over everything else. Gary's assessment reveals he would probably not be good as a human resources director or administrator.

There is no right or wrong assessment. However, it is very useful to know the different personality types on your team so you can put them in the right job. This will go a long way in setting them up for success, not failure, and help you work with them in the right way to bring out their best.

ROCKET FUEL

Another way to look at the concept of "right people in the right seats" is how the book *Rocket Fuel* breaks it down. At the top, you need a visionary, someone who creates the overall plan for the business. This cannot be the person that is doing everything, as the visionary needs time to work on the overall trajectory of the business rather than be consumed by day-to-day work. This is critical for success.

But you also need an integrator, someone who takes the vision, generally created by the head of the company, and sees it through. This person thrives on creating order out of chaos. He or she is naturally suited to setting priorities, solving conflicts, removing obstacles, and getting the company from point A to point B. You can't only have visionaries on your team, and you can't only have integrators. You need both. Integrators don't necessarily have to be business partners, so you can hire for this role, as the book suggests.

OBSTACLES TO TEAM BUILDING

Despite the obvious benefits of building a team, we've found that several Asset Managers don't take the plunge. One big obstacle to hiring a team is money. Perhaps you are thinking, "*Gary and Kyle, I do not have enough money to pay someone.*" We get it; we have been there ourselves. Try to team up with someone who has a different skillset. This is an effective way of establishing the benefits of a team without hiring. Or you could pay someone an incentive-based pay and share in the profits. There are always solutions, and as a successful Asset Manager, you must have that mindset.

Also remember we are not saying go out and hire a whole team suddenly. You must manage your cash flow, or it will sink you. I have seen far too many businesses get too far ahead of themselves. Like anything, moderation is key. Test, tweak, improve. Test, tweak, improve. As we mentioned, building a team takes time. You must be patient.

VIRTUAL ASSISTANTS

Virtual assistants can be a great asset to any team. Typically, the cost is very low, and they are independent contractors, saving you payroll taxes. They provide their own equipment, and you do not have to provide office space. You have the flexibility to hire them for one-off jobs, very specific ongoing tasks, or full time, if you have the need for it. Virtual assistants are a great option for organizations of any size.

MANAGING YOUR TEAM

Once you have a team in place, it's important to manage them effectively to get the best results. Truth is, if someone is not invested in your company—and I do not mean that in the literal sense—they will not go that extra mile. Sometimes, their 85 percent may be good enough, but if you can find what motivates that person and get their full 100 percent, that's golden. Here are some principles and processes we find valuable for team management.

HIRE SLOW, FIRE FAST

One of the key principles of building and managing your team is to hire slow and fire fast. By "hire slow," we mean you need to take your time to find the right person for the specific role you are hiring for. It's also important to make sure they fit your organization's culture. Take your time to choose teammates with complementary skills and create a diverse team with multiple viewpoints.

It's equally important to "fire fast." Here's what we mean by this: if you have an employee that isn't performing up to your standards, you must first make sure you have set that person up for success. Have you given them all the tools they need and communicated all your expectations upfront? Have you provided feedback on their results? If you have done these things and they are *still* not meeting the performance levels you have set up for them, it is best that you let this person go, and do it quickly.

When we say "fire fast," we mean it's important not to dillydally on this decision once you've made it. An under-performer can bring your team down, and conversely, a high performer raises everyone's game. Who would you rather have on your team? Waiting many months for someone to up their game will only give you headaches. That is why "fire fast" is important if someone is not living up to expectations.

BUILDING THE RIGHT CULTURE

It is also important to build the right culture. Do not keep "you" and "them" completely separate. We have seen great results by sharing in team wins and working through struggles together. This builds camaraderie. If you keep your team happy and let each person grow as you grow, they will be problem solvers and not problem creators.

Also, make sure you get to know your team. There are many ways to foster relationships: grab a meal, play golf, go to an event together, etc. It should not all just be about business. Get to really know the person you are working with. What are they passionate about? What are their triggers? How do they like to be spoken to? If you know these things about a person, it is easier to have them on your side, which helps build strong relationships.

STRUCTURING INCENTIVES

Another good way to build strong relationships and keep the team happy is how you structure your incentives. We have seen incentives go well, and we have seen incentives go poorly. The key is to have a motivated team that is all in. With incentives, this means there is big upside for them if the company does well. As Asset Manager, would you rather have a 50 percent share of a well-oiled organization and not have to grind it out 24/7? Or would you prefer to have 75 percent of a smaller pie and not have any time to enjoy it because you're dealing with every single issue that comes up?

We prefer to have a smaller piece of a larger pie with people we can trust and rely on. With good incentives, employees will stay a lot longer. This allows us to build consistency and efficiency, and the business performs at a much higher level!

DELEGATION

Many people struggle with delegation. They think only they can do it the *right* way, and it slows them down. They take on too many tasks and are not able to excel at any of them. You must be able to delegate in this business; there is just too much that must get done.

If you struggle with delegation, here's a simple way to start thinking about it positively. What tasks are highly repetitive? What tasks may cost you twenty dollars an hour for someone else to do? Figure out what you want to ultimately get paid in a year and break that down to weekly and hourly. Seriously—do that right now.

Say you want to make $520,000 a year. Divide that by fifty-two weeks; that comes to $10,000 a week. I know a lot of people that work more than forty hours in a week and a lot of people who work less, but let us say for the sake of this exercise that you work forty hours in a week. That comes to $250 an hour.

Under this scenario, you should aim to delegate any task that costs under $250 an hour. It may take some time to get used to that, so try to start with delegating any task costing under fifty dollars an hour. As you continue to grow your company, use this thought process to keep delegating.

GIVE UP CONTROL

This last principle is less about managing your team and more about managing yourself. Yes, you. Asset Managers are often leaders and visionaries, and that can make it hard for us to give up control. But if you want your business to thrive, you have to be open to things being done in different ways. A team member may not do something as good as you or exactly how you would, but that has got to be okay. You may be surprised when you give someone latitude to perform a task and they do it better than you imagined. That is the best outcome, right?

VENDORS

Building your team also includes people outside your organization; this is your external team. You may have third-party property managers, contractors, and vendors helping you. When it comes to selecting these team members, it is always good to get referrals from others to help you get started.

When we were starting out, we asked brokers which third-party property management companies they liked. We met with these companies and got them involved when we were interested in a property. We toured the property with them, discussed the business plan, and had the property management companies create a pro forma. (A pro forma will lay out projected income and expenses so you can evaluate future performance for a property.) You want to develop a relationship where it is okay to debate. You don't want someone to just be a "yes man" and tell you they can get you a specific rent number that is too aggressive—because if they cannot deliver on that business plan, you are not going to be in business long.

The property management company you choose will help you set rents, tell you what renovation level is best for that submarket and what amenities you need, and more. These are all things you also need to figure out on your own by visiting comps; it's important to stay knowledgeable and involved in your properties. But if you can build trust with a company such that you know the value of their advice and figures, it will help you immensely.

Once you have a good property management company in place, things become a little easier. For example, you may not have to spend time vetting each and every one of your vendors, as your third-party property manager probably can recommend a few for each category. That being said, you want to make sure you get multiple bids for any work needed.

As we wrote earlier, building a quality team takes time, and it will evolve based on your business needs. Do not skimp on the time it takes to get the right people in the right seats. Hiring the most qualified employees/vendors will save you time and headaches. I'm sure you heard this many times before, but it really is true: real estate is a team sport. It is impossible to be an expert in everything, and if you expect to scale, you need to rely on others. Strong internal and external teams will help you become a Best in Class Asset Manager and hopefully triple your income like Tim Bratz.

A great resource for vendors is our Facebook Group: Asset Management Mastery We have members from all over the world that are willing and able to help each other out.

Here is a list of some team members you may want to think about working with:

- Acquisitions Manager
- Certified Public Accountant (CPA)
- Electrician
- General Contractor

- Insurance Broker
- Lender
- Local Bank
- Plumber
- Property Manager
- Real Estate Transaction Attorney
- Roofer
- Signage Specialist
- Syndication Attorney
- Underwriter
- Virtual Assistant
- Water Conservation Specialist

CHAPTER 3

DUE DILIGENCE

Diligence is not easy, but we can't reach our goals without it.

—HENRY CLOUD

Due diligence is one of the most critical steps in buying a property. This is your opportunity to look under the hood, so to speak, and find what may be wrong with the property or what may become a problem in the future. This is your chance to inspect everything—and we mean *everything*! Thorough due diligence is a lot of work, and at the end of the day, you may end up walking away from the deal. Nevertheless, always be as detailed as you can during the due-diligence process; you owe it to yourself and your investors.

In this chapter, we are going to focus on due diligence after you have an accepted offer. By this stage, you should have already analyzed the property's twelve-month statement (also known as the Trailing 12 or T12), the rent roll, and the submarket; underwritten the deal; and come up with a business plan, at the very least. This is how we like to look at deals. Once you have these steps under your belt, here's what you need to know about the due diligence process and how to approach it.

THE BASICS: TIMING, REPORTS, BEST PRACTICES

In an ideal world, the broker and owner should disclose everything about the property, but we would not count on it. If you find things that are wrong during the due diligence process—and you will—remember, that is okay. Every property has a price. If a property is perfect, you will pay a price that reflects that perfection, and if it is not, you will pay a price that reflects its actual condition.

When you start the due diligence process is important. You want to start due diligence as soon as possible to give yourself the biggest window of time to find any issues, get bids, and make an informed decision. Sometimes, in a hot market, when you have put hard money down on day one, you should ask to get access to the property to start due diligence while you are working on the contract. This request is important when you are condensing your due diligence period but does not matter otherwise.

Due diligence periods can be as little as zero days and as long as sixty days. It depends on how hot the market is and how badly you want to beat out a competing offer. You can typically do almost everything you need to do in the first thirty days (although the longer the timeframe you can get, the more protected you are). A property survey, environmental report, and full title report could take thirty to sixty-plus days.

PROPERTY SURVEY

A property survey is a document that shows the property lines—including any land, structures, and features involved in the sale—as a schematic diagram of angles and measurements. A property survey is not mandatory, but it would identify any issues with property lines, easements, zoning classifications, ingress, and egress. It is a small cost for something that could identify a potential problem down the road.

ENVIRONMENTAL REPORT

An environmental report identifies potential or existing environmental contamination liabilities. It is usually required by lenders. If they find something wrong in the initial report (i.e., the Phase 1 report), a Phase 2 Environmental Site Assessment or a Phase II Environmental Report is done. This is a direct test on underground materials to check for possible contamination. The process entails drilling at sites with recognizable environmental conditions (RECs) and is a lot costlier than a Phase 1 report. If your site has to go into a Phase 2 analysis, you may have to walk away from the deal due to the cost (it depends on if you are working with a seller that is going to be flexible).

TITLE REPORT

A title report discloses the rightful owner and vesting interests in the property, as well as details of liens, encroachments, and easements. We recommend having both you and your transactional attorney review this report to ensure you understand any potential red flags and issues. You would want to clear these up before purchasing the property.

Apart from a property survey, environmental report, and title report, you may also need an appraisal and property condition assessment (PCA), though they can usually be done within your thirty-day timeframe.

APPRAISAL

An appraisal is done by a third-party professional to get an estimation of the market and land value of the property you are looking to purchase. The in-depth analysis not only covers the property but the market as well.

PROPERTY CONDITION ASSESSMENT

Insurance, commercial mortgage-backed securities (CMBS), and some portfolio lenders require a PCA, also known as a property condition report (PCR). These assessments cover all major building systems and site improvements. They also include a replacement reserve and immediate repairs table that identifies capital needs for failing or damaged building systems. These reports are very lengthy—our last one was over 1,100 pages!

While the reports are being ordered, you will perform unit interior inspections, lease audits/operations inspections, and exterior inspections as part of your due diligence. (These will be covered in more detail later in this chapter.) Make sure you schedule these inspections with your third-party property management team, plumber, electrician, roofer, general contractor, pest control specialist, heating ventilation and air conditioning (HVAC) contractor, and any other subcontractor you may need.

If your third-party property management company does not perform due diligence inspections, you should hire a company to help you. This is a big undertaking, and you want someone who has done this countless times on your side. Remember, this is your one opportunity to make sure you know what you are buying.

When it comes to due diligence, you want to be as thorough

as possible on your first shot to save time. However, you may uncover something you need to bring a specialist back for. Do not hesitate to bring two or three vendors, like roofers, in for the same issue, but at different times, of course, because you often get different solutions and prices when they are brought in separately. One may say you need a whole new roof, and another may say you only need to do some patch work and you'll be good for a number of years. Having a third company will help clarify what work you really need and how much it should cost.

You should ask for any environmental surveys, appraisals, utility bills, bank statements, and real estate tax documents the seller may have. Be sure to look at the insurance loss runs, as these may identify challenges the property has had in the past and allow you to get them checked out.

You will also want updated financials and rent rolls throughout the process until you close. It is very important the property's financials do not slip before closing to ensure the best loan terms and proceeds. Additionally, it is good to have consistent communication and transparency with your lender during this entire process to ensure there are no major hiccups with the loan.

THE PROCESS: DETAIL AND DOCUMENT!

Once you are on the property and actually conducting due diligence, you and your team will inspect everything:

- The entranceway
- Parking lot
- Curbs
- Roof
- Landscaping
- Rain gutters and downspouts
- Exterior stucco or paint
- Electrical panel, light switches, and power outlets
- Thermostats and HVAC system
- Plumbing fixtures, faucets, and water heater
- Leaks
- Appliances
- Walls, ceilings, and floors
- Doors and windows
- Stairs, steps, and railings
- Porches and balconies
- Walkways
- Mold
- And many other things!

You will also get a report from each third-party company you hire about these inspections. Make sure you go over it with a fine-toothed comb. Based on the findings of these inspections and the recommendations of the report, you may need to go back to the seller and discuss a new price, tweak your business plan, and/or work with your lender regarding holdbacks. It is therefore important to have tremendous attention to detail at this stage. If you miss anything, you may pay the price later. However, keep in mind you cannot go back to the seller for little things. These small things should have been built into your budget, particularly in a seller's market. The rule of thumb is that you should only go back for items that have not been disclosed prior to your offer being accepted.

During the due diligence process, **you**—along with the help of others on your team if it's a large property—will need to walk *every* unit. We do mean every unit because you never know what you are going to find. We bolded "you" because you need to be there. It is a big decision to buy a property, particularly if investors are involved, and you need to be there to have eyes on everything that gets uncovered. Reading a report is helpful, but if you are the Asset Manager, you better be there for the inspections.

Be wary if the seller does not let you see certain units. We suggest you demand to see them if you want to be 100 percent sure they are in good condition. Your goal in due diligence is to leave no stone unturned. Don't be afraid to push back if you feel there is something not being disclosed.

Lastly, make sure your third-party company makes a list of

every unit that includes the unit number, the condition of every item and appliance in the unit, and any other notes. It's necessary to include this level of detail per unit because the minutia will vary from unit to unit. Pictures are also good to have. They will come in handy when you are doing your rehab, as you will have a general reference for what condition the unit was in initially.

LEASE AUDITS

Once you have done your due diligence on the property, there is still work to be done. You and the property management company (or third-party company) will need to do a lease audit. You want to make sure your residents are qualified during the lease audit, which means they are able to pay rent. Sometimes, property management companies stuff the place with residents that do not have a monthly income more than two and a half times the monthly rent just to keep the occupancy high during the sale. By performing a lease audit, you or the company you hire should be able to identify this. It is not necessarily a dealbreaker, but it is nice to know what you are getting into if you do decide to move forward with the deal. Cities vary on what defines creditworthy, but having your net monthly income at least two and a half times your rent gives the owner confidence you are most likely able to cover all your bills and rent.

You will also want to know:

- When is each lease up?
- What is each tenant currently paying in rent and does it match their lease?
- What are they charging for ratio utility billing system (RUBS), if anything?
- Are all leases signed?
- Do any tenants have criminal records?
- Are there special exceptions to leases?
- Are there a large number of residents delinquent on rent?
- Were there credit checks performed on potential tenants?
- Are there too many people living in any unit?
- Are they charging month-to-month charges for expired leases?
- How many leases are month to month?
- Are security deposits collected, and how much?
- Are they charging late fees?
- Are they charging pet fees?

It is tedious work, but it must get done no matter how many units there are.

UTILITY BILLS

You will want to review utility bills to identify opportunities or red flags. You may even want to go back two to three years, not just twelve months. That way, you can identify any trends that have not been disclosed. Is the bill too high compared to other properties that have the same number of units in the area? If so, why? Is there more grass/landscaping to water; could there be a leak somewhere? You can hire a company to do a utility audit in order to track billing errors and evaluate rate plans to make suggestions for further savings. You can also have an energy audit done, which will advise you on how to minimize energy spending through increased efficiencies.

Going through utility bills is not exciting, but there is a lot of opportunity that can be found here. If you can save $500 per month, multiply that by twelve months and divide by a 6 cap, you just created $100,000 of value in your property. That may not seem like much to some Asset Managers (savings can be significantly more depending on the size of your property), but a little bit of due diligence goes a long way in strengthening returns for you and your investors. And conversely, it can cost you if you don't pay attention. You'll want to confirm the utilities listed on the T12 actually match the bills. If not, you need to adjust your underwriting to match the actual bills.

This is also a good time to identify utility deposits; this number can be substantial depending on the size of the property you are buying. You want to make sure you have accounted for all the money you need to be well capitalized when you take over a property.

CONTRACTS

You will want to review all the contracts the previous owner made for the property, such as laundry, trash pickup, exterminator, landscaping, Wi-Fi, snow removal (depending on location), or cable. When do these contracts expire? Are there hidden fees in the agreements? Is canceling them even an option, or are you stuck with the contracts until they expire? Did the seller get a one-time lump-sum fee, and if so, are you getting a pro rata share of that fee? If you are planning on adding washers and dryers to units, you'll need to check if the laundry contract allows that. Attention to detail is time consuming but necessary. Are there escalator fees in the contracts? You may be stuck with a contract you do not like for a period of time, which may affect your underwriting. You can try to renegotiate a contract you do not like based on leverage from another bidder and potentially save a lot of money when you take over. Additionally, you may be able to sign a new contract worth upwards of tens of thousands of dollars!

Does your property require any licenses or permits? If so, verify all licenses and permits are in the current owner's name and whether a transfer is required into your property ownership name. Also, check that all licenses and permits are up to date.

COMPS

This is the time to walk the comps again. Many of the reports you pull from Rentometer, CoStar, or the like include apartment buildings that are too far away to be an accurate comparison to the one you're considering or have outdated information. Real estate is hyperlocal, and you want to be looking at apartment buildings next door or down the street that are similar to yours. You want to compare apples to apples. Note that, depending on your market, the distance between similar properties will vary. We're not suggesting a certain perimeter you patrol in. What we mean when we say "compare apples to apples" is you should ensure the comp you are walking through is like the property you are purchasing. It does not make sense to have a comp that is a 200-unit, 2000 build with all the bells and whistles for amenities if you are buying a fifty-unit, 1975 build with no amenities. These properties will attract completely different clientele. Once you have identified the right comps, walk these complexes to review amenities, unit interiors, and all upgrades. This will allow you to understand what your competition is doing so you can tweak your business plan accordingly.

Performing comps at this stage will allow you to also get a better sense of the area. What does the community look like? Is it thriving, or are there a lot of rundown buildings or stores? What do the cars look like, and what about the traffic? Go at different times of the day and days of the week.

We know this can be time consuming, but you are considering purchasing this building! Make sure you put in the work; you owe it to your investors. We hope you checked all of this out beforehand, but just in case you have not reviewed it, now would be a great time.

REASSESS

After you've completed your due diligence, now's the time to reassess. Does the property still make sense? Go back to your underwriting spreadsheet and input any numbers that need to be adjusted. Do you need to build more bad debt or delinquency into your underwriting model based on the lease audit findings? Are repairs more than you budgeted for? Maybe you uncovered fewer units were upgraded than expected, or maybe you found more upgraded units than anticipated (it happens; we received a pleasant surprise on one of our purchases when we found a few more upgraded units than we initially predicted).

If things need to be fixed, make sure you get multiple bids. It is not always about the lowest price. You want it fixed right the first time to avoid headaches in the future. Based on due diligence, do you think the lender will require repairs that you have not accounted for? This is called an immediate repairs list (IRL), and the lender will hold back money until those items are fixed, so make sure you are prepared for that. There is no escaping this for agency lenders, so if it's not in your budget, you will have no choice but to add it.

Now that you have updated your underwriting spreadsheet, does the purchase of the property still make sense? Has the deal changed to the degree that you need to go back to the buyer and request a change in price? There is no hard and fast rule for when you should do this. Obviously, sellers and brokers want to work with someone that will close without any issues and frown upon re-trading. But there are times you must have that discussion if new information has changed the deal. It is tougher to get concessions in a seller's market, but you do have one advantage: they are probably reluctant to start the selling process over again with another buyer and waste valuable time. As we mentioned before, be reasonable about asking for concessions; you cannot ask for minor things that come up. It needs to be something that was not disclosed and has an effect on your returns.

CONCLUSION

Meticulous due diligence is the start of excellent asset management. It is crucial you take the time to do this part well and remember to utilize a team. You do not need to be an expert inspector, but you do need to be organized and manage the experts on your team. This critical piece is setting your investment up to minimize expenses and maximize income, which means greater profit and value for your property.

Visit www.bestinclassbook.co for our Due Diligence Checklist.

CHAPTER 4

BUDGETING

A goal without a plan is just a wish.

—ANONYMOUS

Budgeting is essentially your underwriting for a property and should be done well in advance of closing. There is a slight difference between budgeting and underwriting: underwriting is your initial pass at your business plan and assumptions, while budgeting is where you really dig into your business plan and think things through on a month-over-month and year-over-year basis. Your business plan is a fluid, living thing, and you may need to pivot and adjust your plan based on the market and the performance of the property, which means your budget for certain things will change as well.

As always, we do not suggest relying solely on your property management company to build out your budget for each year. Your input is crucial, as you have the most knowledge of your business plan and how it needs to be executed to achieve your goals. Your property management company's input in your budgeting process is, however, very important and will help you get on the right track. You will want to have a conversation with them about your plan and whether each item is achievable or unrealistic. Once we have our initial budget set (and the property under contract), we have a detailed meeting with the property management team to go over final costs for things such as payroll, renovations, utilities, etc., to make sure we are dialed in.

When it comes to budgeting, every property and business plan are different and so is every market. Each property will present itself with different challenges. Therefore, we will not be covering specific assumptions you should be taking into consideration here but rather the thought process and mindset behind them. We will also not be covering any type of debt or exit assumptions in this chapter. We will cover exit assumptions in Chapter 16, when we discuss disposition.

GET INTO THE DETAILS

Budgeting is not just about getting your year one projections locked in and then building in a static percentage increase across the board for the remainder of the hold—

which, by the way, many Asset Managers do. It is always a best practice to think about where the property will be in the future. Do you need a full staff in every year of the hold? Or do you need to be heavily staffed during the stabilization/value-add phase and can temper off once that phase is complete? Can you implement a utility savings plan, and when will that plan be complete enough for you to start realizing those savings? Budgeting is peeling back the onion a few layers further and really digging into each line item to think about how your business plan will affect it. In some cases, your business plan may increase certain expense items. For example, if your plan is to re-tenant the property after you have done most of the exterior renovations and fixed the deferred maintenance, your marketing budget may increase in years two to three to produce more leads and traffic and only then come back down. Having a straight 3 percent increase across the board would not make sense in this situation. The same goes for other income items. If you plan on adding covered parking or charging for additional amenities like a package locker but will not install them until all renovations are complete, income from these amenities would not be added until possibly year two or three.

Having flat percentage increases across the board is a mistake. It shows you have not thoroughly thought through your business plan. Remember, the business plan is for the life of the hold, not just year one. If you wait until after you own the property to think about the future years, it will likely be too late. It is much more difficult to make adjustments on the fly than it is to anticipate them in advance. For example, if you planned on a straight increase in your insurance costs of 3 percent annually and they shoot up 5 percent, where else can you really save from that overage? You are now in a position where the likely place to make that up is the income lines. Can you push income any more, or were you too aggressive there as well? Will you push anyway and see if you can get just a little more rent? Did your occupancy drop because you were too aggressive? Did your turnover increase? As you can see, this can start to snowball. It's extremely difficult to find solid ground and get back on track once this begins. You owe it to your investors to think about the business plan in full and through disposition.

Also, do not make the mistake of creating your budget and then forgetting about it. What we mean by this is budgets are typically drawn out for the course of the entire hold period upfront. So if it's a five-year hold, all five years are done prior to closing on the property. Adjusting the budget on a yearly basis based on current performance and new expectations—whether good or bad—is a necessary process and should involve your property management company.

CAPEX AND RESERVES

In addition to your initial budget and your year-over-year budget, you also have to manage your capex, or renovation, budget along with your reserves budget. You will want to track each item/project separately. Make sure you keep an eye on where you are in terms of overspending or savings. This is the only way you will know if you need to adjust other items you planned for or have some excess funds to distribute. If you were conservative in your initial underwriting, the hope would be you have plenty of funds in reserve for a rainy day. Spending money like a drunken sailor until it runs out and then deciding what to do will not end well. You don't need any fancy tool here; this can all be tracked in Excel or Google Sheets. Regardless of the tool you use, you need to know your cash position and how it relates to your business plan.

Reserves are typically held in an escrow account by the lender along with the items they outlined in the IRL. These funds are set aside to be used for certain projects, and you will need to manage the timing and use of these funds. This is typical for any agency loan; if you are working with private capital, insurance groups, or local banks, their requirements may be different. You don't always have enough in the reserves for the specific projects laid out in the IRL, so you may need to work with the lender a bit to decide how to manage this and where to best spend the money. For example, you may have HVAC, roof, and parking lot replacement scheduled for year three. If you do not have enough in the reserves to cover all these items, it's best to communicate with the lender early and work with them to decide which ones make more sense to postpone until your reserve funds can cover the costs.

BUSINESS PLANS CHANGE

Always look ahead (be proactive) and think about the things that need to happen now in order to produce a certain result in the future. A great example of this is our first property in Tucson, Arizona. It took us less time than we anticipated to stabilize the property, and we were able to push rents higher than we originally thought. At that point, we decided to get the broker we purchased it from to give us his thoughts on our business plan; we wanted to know if we should pivot since we were well ahead of schedule. (We like to list a property with the broker from whom we purchased it; this business is about relationships, and this goes a long way in establishing trust with the brokers.) This particular broker met us at the property and was impressed with the results we were getting so far. He suggested we implement a new premium-level unit to see what kind of rents we could get and what the cost to upgrade the unit would be. It ended up being a great return on investment and plan for us. This led us to implementing five premium units and listing the property for sale five years earlier than planned!

If you just try to stick to the plan and not continue to look for opportunities, they will definitely pass you by. We tell this story not to boast but because we had to adjust our budget and be sure we were making the right decisions for the property and our investors. We had to pull the additional funds needed to build out the new premium units from somewhere, whether it be cash flow (which we do not suggest), other projects in the budget, contingency funds, or, in our case, funds that ended up not being used on other projects. Regardless, the process is the same. You need to evaluate the budget and available funds to make the best decision for the property.

On the other side of this, you may find the property is just not performing the way you would like and/or you've had to spend additional dollars in other areas, such as unplanned deferred maintenance, security due to increased crime, or busted water lines. In these cases, you may have to make decisions about your budget and business plan that are not going to be easy. When in doubt on what to do, it is always best to ask others that have been in your situation before. Your property management company is certainly a good place to start, but also use other investors in your network and market as resources. You never know what information you will find. We have had several instances where we asked for and received a helping hand that showed us how to navigate a situation.

We have a property where we did not plan on or budget

for a full paint job. The paint was in good shape when we bought the property, so we were only going to do a partial paint and add highlights to change the look and feel of the property slightly. After we closed and received feedback from several potential and current residents as well as our property management company, we decided a full paint job was needed to update the property and give it a new, modern look. This ended up costing us about $60,000 more than we budgeted. Luckily, we had a large reserve and contingency account to pull from. This was not an easy decision to make and definitely impacted our business plan. After a long discussion with our team and the property management company, we felt it was the right decision for the property; it was needed to separate ourselves from our competition. The new paint colors also resulted in better visibility from the street, as the old colors blended in too much. The goal was to increase demand for our units, enabling us to charge higher rents, so we felt the paint job would more than pay for itself.

CONCLUSION

Nothing about asset management is sexy, but it is where all the money is made—or lost, for that matter. Building out a well-thought-out, detailed budget can take a lot of time and energy. But in the end, you will thank yourself for thinking through all the minor details in advance. It will also make you a better investor and Asset Manager!

CHAPTER 5

FINANCIAL ANALYSIS

Analysis is the critical starting point of strategic thinking.

—KENICHI OHMAE

Financial analysis is the process of evaluating your businesses, projects, budgets, and other finance-related transactions to determine their performance and suitability. Typically, in multifamily real estate, financial analysis is used to analyze whether a property is stable or profitable enough to warrant an investment. Financial analysis, however, is not only required in the upfront evaluation of a property but also needs to be done on an ongoing basis— you could consider it general maintenance, if you will.

In order to fully understand the health of your business or your property, you must understand the financial analysis side of things. If you do not understand this side, you will find making the right decisions regarding the direction of your property tougher. These decisions tend to build on one another and will begin to snowball in the right or wrong direction, so let's make sure you are on the right side of that snowball. Financial analysis has a lot to do with digging into the numbers, identifying trends, and spotting things that just don't look right. The first thing you'll need to know is what each financial report represents and how you should be looking at it. Let's go over some of these reports.

BALANCE SHEET

A balance sheet is a financial statement that reports a property's assets, liabilities, and capital balance at a specific point in time. It provides a basis for computing rates of return and evaluating the property's capital structure. Each of the three segments on the balance sheet will have many accounts within it that document the value of each. Accounts such as operating cash, prepaid expenses, accounts receivable, and reserves are on the asset side of the balance sheet, while on the liability side there are accounts such as accounts payable, accrued expenses, and long-term debt. The capital balance will be the net of your assets minus your liabilities.

Key items to keep an eye on in the balance sheet are your operating cash and accounts receivable/payable. Accounts payable is the money the property owes its vendors, and accounts receivable is the amount owed to the property. If not properly accounted for and attended to, your balance sheet can become very "out of balance," and the property's actual performance can essentially be hidden within these accounts. Make sure to understand these accounts, and ensure the balances make sense and are not piling up. For samples of the reports we mention in this chapter, go to www.bestinclassbook.co.

CASH FLOW STATEMENT

The cash flow statement makes adjustments to the information recorded on your income statement to show your net cash flow (income minus expenses)—the precise amount of cash you have on hand for that time period, usually for a given month and also year to date. Or, in some cases, it shows the amount of cash you lost for that time period.

You should break down the cash flow statement a bit further and look into each of the income and expense line items to identify anything that seems out of the ordinary. Since the cash flow statement is just a summary of each account, you will have to go one step further in your analysis: you will need to use the general ledger to dig in a little deeper. We will get to the general ledger shortly.

BUDGET COMPARISON

A budget comparison report is exactly what it sounds like. It compares your actual income, expenses, NOI, cash flow, etc., to your budgeted income and expenses. This allows you to compare the areas where the property is exceeding expectations with other areas where you may need improvement. Having something to compare to is always good when analyzing your financials, as it gives you a starting point. Make sure if you are a value-add investor, you take this into account when building your budget during the value-add phase. Having a budget that is evenly distributed by taking the total and dividing it by twelve may work once a property is stabilized, but during the value-add phase, you will want the budget to be thought out more on a month-over-month basis, with a steady increase as you stabilize.

You will never find a budget comparison where everything is exactly how you planned it. Your job is to identify the areas where the property is struggling and put a plan in place to get those items fixed.

TWELVE-MONTH STATEMENT (TRAILING 12 OR T12)

The twelve-month statement is your cash flow statement for the last twelve-month period. This report is one you will use to identify negative and positive trends over time since you are looking at a snapshot of the property's performance over the last year. Many of the items in this report will also be used to create the KPIs we'll cover in Chapter 8. When calculating a property's value, the T12 NOI is often a starting point. You will need to monitor this report and the KPIs generated from it to create better consistency across all areas of your property's performance.

GENERAL LEDGER

A general ledger represents the recordkeeping system for a property's financial data, with debit and credit account records validated by a trial balance. The general ledger provides a record of each financial transaction that takes place during the life of an operating company (in our case, the property). As mentioned above, this is where you can dive in and identify exactly where your money is flowing in and out and where you will need to look to see each transaction. This is where the most details lie and what you should be looking at if something seems out of the ordinary. You will want to spend some time each month in the general ledger to make sure things are properly accounted for.

ACCOUNTS RECEIVABLE AND PAYABLE

Accounts receivable is the balance of money due but not yet paid for by residents; this is listed on the balance sheet as an asset. Accounts payable are amounts due to vendors or suppliers for goods or services received that have not yet been paid for; this is listed on the balance sheet as a liability. Much like the cash flow statement, the receivables and payables listed in the balance sheet are just a summary. If your balances in these accounts start to inflate, you will want to keep an eye on the aged reports for a more detailed look. Typically, the aging report will break down what is owed for the current period: zero to thirty days, thirty-one to sixty days, sixty-one to ninety days, and more than ninety days. If you are seeing balances that are over sixty days, you will definitely want to ask your property management company about them. This could be an issue where the property management company is pushing off paying any bills to hide the actual performance of the property and (as in some cases we have seen) hit their quarterly bonus with their company.

BANK RECONCILIATION STATEMENT

The purpose of a bank reconciliation statement is to detect any discrepancies between the accounting records of the property and the bank, besides those due to normal timing differences. Such discrepancies might exist due to an error on the part of the property management company or the bank. You will want to make sure your property management company provides this statement to you on a monthly basis in order to catch errors, avoid surprises, save money, verify cash flow, and, essentially, prevent fraud.

I am sure you are asking yourself, "Can I just hire a CPA

or accountant to do this?" Yes, you can; in fact, this is something we highly encourage. However, that CPA or accountant does not know the property like you do and will not be able to identify everything that is out of place. A CPA or accountant is there as a *second* set of eyes and to balance the accounts, but you need to be the first set of eyes to make sure everything is in order. We once found a $10,000 charge for a plumbing expense that was not for our property (even our manager missed it). Had we not audited our financials on a monthly basis, we would have been responsible for that expense.

Property management companies have large portfolios they manage, and their accountants are in charge of multiple properties, so there can be mistakes made. You need to be another set of eyes. You must question charges that look to be out of place and/or unexpected. If you are new to looking at reports like this, you may want someone on your team with this experience. If you can't afford to hire someone to your team, you will need to dedicate the time and energy necessary to learn these reports very well. It may seem difficult at first, but over time, you will improve.

If you are not auditing your financials, you are certainly leaving money on the table. Also, do not make the mistake of only looking at line items that are over budget. There have been many times when the cash flow statement looked fine, but after digging into the general ledger, we found expenses that were either double charged, coded incorrectly, or not supposed to be there. As you will find out in Chapter 16 (on dispositions), everything needs to be lined up for you to get the most value for your property. If items are being coded to incorrect accounts, that could have an effect on the buyer's proceeds from the lender.

A great example of this is an asset management fee. Do you throw this in with the property management account or payroll, or is it below the NOI line? Technically, this is not a property operating expense and so should be below the NOI line. That way, it does not affect the NOI or any calculations from the lender's side. This small change can have a large impact on value. If your asset management fee is $30,000 per year and calculated at a 6 cap, that represents a $500,000 difference in value. Dialing in how and where things are coded is just as important as anything else when it comes to financial analysis.

CASH VERSUS ACCRUAL ACCOUNTING METHOD

A key part of financial analysis is understanding the different accounting methods. For the most part, you will see property management companies and owners operating under an accrual accounting method. However, there are those that prefer the cash accounting method. It is important to understand the difference between the two, as it does affect month-to-month cash flows and reporting.

The main difference between accrual and cash accounting comes down to the timing of when revenue and expenses are recognized. The cash method is a more immediate recognition of revenue and expenses, while the accrual method focuses on anticipated revenue and expenses. Let's consider, as an example, rent collections. In the cash method, if you have residents who are paying for their June rent at the end of May, those revenues would actually be accounted for in the month of May, even though the rent is for June. This essentially inflates the revenues for May and deflates them for June. This is why you will mainly see accrual accounting being used. This is also a huge factor to consider when underwriting deals, as the T12 and T3 will likely show larger swings if the cash method was used.

CONCLUSION

Ultimately, financial analysis is about understanding the overall health of your property and your cash position. Without knowing these things, you will be making decisions in the dark. When you have this understanding, you can quickly identify and resolve challenges and even take advantage of potential opportunities. One of the main components of being a great Asset Manager is the ability to shed light on everything so you can make clear, educated decisions. The first step is educating yourself or adding someone to your team who is knowledgeable in financial analysis. Without it, you could be costing yourself and your investors time and money.

CHAPTER 6

LEGAL

A law is valuable, not because it is a law, but because there is right in it.

—HENRY WARD BEECHER

We are not going to dig into the legal side of things too much, as we are not attorneys (nor do we want to be!). The whole reason you hire an attorney is so you don't have to read one of those long, drawn-out boilerplate documents, right? The biggest takeaway you can get from this chapter is to have an attorney on your team. More likely than not, you will have *more* than one. If you do syndications like we do, you will need a Securities and Exchange Commission (SEC) attorney to draft your private placement memorandum (PPM) docs and keep you compliant with the SEC. You will also need a real estate transactions attorney to help advise you on all contracts outside of the SEC filings, such as the purchase and sale agreement. If we were to take it a step further, you may also want an asset protection attorney on your team.

KNOW YOUR PPM

As you should already know, the PPM is the legal document provided to your prospective investors that describes the company selling the securities, the terms of the offering, and the risks of the investment, among other things. The PPM, in and of itself, is kind of worthless—you can just pull one from the internet or use a template. It's what you put *into* the PPM that's important. And you should be working very closely with your SEC attorney to make sure all the information in the PPM is written as you intend it to be. For example, the difference between "return *of* capital" and "return *on* capital" is important—and yes, one word can make a huge difference. This particular example has to do with how you pay back your investors and track their capital account/balance. If your capital account/balance is being reduced, this would be considered "return of capital." If you are receiving distributions from cash flow, it is considered "return on capital." If your PPM says one thing and you are doing another, you are not compliant with your documents and, therefore, your offering.

Just as important as making sure the information in the PPM is accurate is understanding the PPM you are providing to your investors and remembering the terms laid out in those documents. Typical syndications hold onto properties for several years, so remembering everything in a PPM is a very difficult thing to do, if not impossible. This is especially the case if you have several offerings over the course of multiple years and have to adjust some of the terms between each offering. It's important, therefore, to keep referring back to your PPM when you are asked a question about your offering by an investor or you are sending out specific communication; this helps ensure you are conveying accurate information and following the guidelines set out in your offering. The PPM is a binding legal document, and you are responsible for making sure you follow it accordingly.

ADVERTISING (APPLIES TO 506(B) OFFERINGS)

If you file your offerings as 506(b), this section is for you! Navigating the fine line between conditioning the market and adding value is something you must be aware of. It is not an easy thing to do. In our opinion, it is always best to err on the side of caution, as you do not want to cross any lines and be on the wrong side of the SEC.

Other than the most obvious form of advertising of a 506(b) offering—which is a blatant act of disregard of the SEC's rules and regulations about advertising—there are generally two types of indirect advertising that will get sponsors in trouble. These types of advertising are not as obvious and can be easy to miss. The first is when you have an active deal, and the second is when you don't have an active deal. Remember, just because you didn't know it was wrong or other people are doing it does not mean you can't get in trouble for it.

The first type is when you indirectly advertise that you have an active deal. This means anything that drums up interest about that deal, even though it's not a specific post or advertisement. For example, you might be talking about due diligence and walking units with your property management company. At this point, you are fine, but then you start bringing up how everybody knows you're raising money. Now you are indirectly advertising for your deal, and this can be considered conditioning the market. Just because you didn't mention *specific* returns and directly ask people to invest does not mean it cannot be considered advertising. Consult with your attorney before posting anything on social media or sending out emails to potential investors.

You also need to be careful of advertising when you don't have an active offering. This is the second type of indirect advertising that gets people into trouble. Most people think that, as long as they do not have a current deal on the table, anything goes when it comes to posting on social media or sending out an email. But there is such a thing as preconditioning the market.

One of the most common forms of preconditioning is the post-closing post. This is the one where everybody celebrates and says, "Hey, super happy to announce that I, my team, and our investors have closed on this amazing property." There are two issues with this:

1. If you're continuing to raise money after you make that post, the deal isn't done! Some people close on the property but still need to raise an additional $50,000 to $100,000 (sometimes more). This may not happen for another week or sometimes even a month. If that's the case, your celebratory post is now considered preconditioning the market. That creates problems for you regarding the money you raise after that post; technically, you've advertised your deal, so that last $50,000 to $100,000 is a violation of 506(b).

2. If you have another deal just around the corner, this could be considered preconditioning the market for that deal as well.

Another example of preconditioning the market would be if you went on a podcast and said, "Hey, we've gone full cycle on several deals. In the past, we've given our investors 15 to 20 percent returns; you should really call us because we know what we are doing." This may seem kind of obvious, but just because you don't have an active deal does not mean you can tell people the types of returns you provide or have provided in the past.

There is a ton of grey area when it comes to advertising. In our opinion, the key is to truly come from a place of adding value to others, not indirectly selling your deal. There is nothing wrong with you making a post on social media that says you wrote an article about why multifamily is the greatest asset class of all time for creating wealth or why Tucson, Arizona, is the greatest market right now. Nor is there anything wrong with hosting a webinar about why real estate is so great. You can do that as long as you are not talking about a specific deal or deals in general. Pure value-add is probably the best way to continue to build your list and talk about real estate with others. Just be careful. Remember, you are going to get somebody's email or contact information from that post, which is great! But then you need to follow the right steps to establish a relationship with the potential investor prior to them investing in your next offering.

ASSET PROTECTION

With regard to asset protection, there are two key points you should keep in mind. First, if you are hiring a third-party property management company, recognize that, as the Asset Manager or owner, you are legally responsible for both the property *and* the acts and omissions of that property manager. Therefore, it is important you add the property management company to your insurance policy. You just never know what will happen, so it is best to plan ahead and make sure you are covered.

Second, you may want to consider setting up a separate entity to handle asset management; this entity would be different from the one that owns your share of the property. Typically, when you do a syndication, you may own a small percentage of the property. You want to make sure your asset management company is different from that ownership company so all the liability is at the level of the asset management company. All situations are different, but this is something to at least look into.

Asset protection is a complex topic: there are layers and layers of actions you can take to protect your property. We don't have the space to cover them all here, but we think the best thing you can do is reach out to an asset protection attorney. Schedule a consult with them so you can explain your specific situation and decide on the best steps for you and your company.

CLOSING OUT YOUR OFFERING

Once you have sold your property, you really want to legally close it out. You can definitely just let it lapse and call it a day, and many go down this route. But if you really want to do it right, you need to take the steps to legally close it down. Each state has a different process where you file some type of dissolution document that officially closes it. Before you do this, however, you will want to make sure you've considered a few things.

- Make sure you have paid all outstanding taxes.
- Keep some reserves for additional charges that may pop up. Most operating agreements actually require you to keep some reserves because you never know when there might be an invoice that crops up.
- Consider getting tail insurance coverage. A tail policy covers you for anything that happens once you have sold the property and closed down the entity. This will cover you for things you may not know about. Just because you sold the property doesn't mean you are no longer responsible for anything. This tail policy covers you for the unforeseen and the unknown.

With regard to Form D (which is the form you file when you start accepting money; you file this in every single state where you have an investor), there is nothing you need to do when closing out your entity. The only thing you will need to close out is the entity in the state in which you are incorporated. There are situations where you may have registered the entity in a different state from the location of the property. We typically wouldn't do that, but it's possible there was a reason why your attorney did. In that case, you have to dissolve the entity wherever you registered it. Typically, however, entities are set up in the state where the property is located.

CONCLUSION

This chapter has covered some of the many things you should consider from a legal perspective; there are a lot more. As we mentioned at the beginning of this chapter, it is best to have multiple attorneys on your team to ensure all your T's are crossed and I's dotted. Attorneys may be expensive, but there is a reason for that—it's better to pay an attorney than pay for a mistake on the back end. And there is a high probability you will sleep better at night with the right team of attorneys on your side.

CHAPTER 7

MANAGING THE MANAGER

Failing to plan is planning to fail.

—ANONYMOUS

Believe it or not, one of the keys to managing the manager is selecting the right property management company. Although we will not get into this in detail in this chapter, be sure you take your time when selecting a property management company. Remember, it can make or break your investment. You want a property management company that aligns with your goals, is flexible in its approach, has infrastructure, utilizes technology, and has extensive experience in the type of asset you are looking to purchase. Meet with the owner, regional manager, and other staff in person. Do not take this step lightly because it could be the difference between a successful deal and one that fails. For a free copy of our *65 Questions to Ask a Property Management Company*, visit www.bestinclassbook.co.

Once you have selected your property management company, you just sit back and let it manage your property, right? Wrong! Managing the manager takes planning and work. It is not an easy task, but applying the guidelines we'll cover in this chapter and building systems to hold the manager accountable will go a long way in getting the property to operate efficiently and executing your business plan. Here are a few things to keep in mind to effectively manage the manager.

PUSH BACK AND BE IN CONTROL

The first thing to remember when managing the manager is this is *your* property (or your company's property), not the property management company's. It is there to support *you* and execute your business plan. Do not be afraid to push back and be in control. Yes, the property managers are the experienced experts, but they do not always have the right answers, and they are often stuck in their ways. Property management can be an archaic business due to its very tight margins and necessary overhead. If you want to see things done differently, you need to communicate your vision to your manager and guide them through the process. Be clear about your expectations, and hold them accountable.

TRUST BUT VERIFY

Trust is important when working with a property management company, but blind trust can be abused. A prudent accountability process is essential. In the end, you usually get what you inspect.

A great example of this is when a unit is being renovated. Let's say you have a unit that you've been told is "complete," but really, there are still a few more touch-up items left to do, and it won't actually be rent ready for two to three days. But, in that two-to-three-day process, the weekend hits, so they actually don't complete the unit until the following week, five days after they told you it was complete. To the property management company, this is not a big deal, as it's just a "couple days." But for the operator or Asset Manager, who is trying to identify bottlenecks and monitor how long each part of the process is taking, it could result in you looking into or being concerned about the wrong thing. You may think it's taking too long to lease, when in reality, the rehab just took longer than you were told. Part of the job of an Asset Manager is identifying bottlenecks and finding solutions to those bottlenecks. If you don't verify what's really happening, it's tough to identify the right issues.

Let's look at another example. Visibility of signage is a key component to driving traffic to your property. In the evenings, it's crucial there is ample lighting throughout the property but also on the signage advertising the property.

Most of the time, property management staff are only on the property during daylight hours. It is not often they will be able to identify issues with the lighting, and they may just assume it works if there are no complaints. It's important to verify your signage is visible and well lit. You may think the signage is just not driving traffic to the leasing office, when in fact, it could be the lighting that is your issue.

MAKE THINGS MEASURABLE AND TRACEABLE

If you can't measure it, you can't manage it. Owning or operating a multifamily property is operating a multimillion-dollar business, and it should be run that way. If you want your business to excel and you want to beat out your competition, you must measure and track the performance of your property in multiple categories. This will allow you to get the information and data you need to make good, solid business decisions. Otherwise, all you are doing is shooting in the dark, and that does no one any good.

It's important to ensure your property management company understands this and makes things measurable and traceable. For example, say your leads for future residents are down, and you ask your property management company what it is going to do to drive more leads. They reply, "We will start marketing more." This is not measurable, traceable, or an acceptable answer. An acceptable answer, and one that is both measurable and traceable, is "We will market on these three platforms, it will cost "x" amount of money, and we will provide a weekly report that tracks the results so we can see which platform is performing the best and what your cost per lead and conversion is." That's the kind of answer you should be pushing for. Again, if you can't measure it, you can't manage it (we will dive deeper into this in the next chapter). Your systems must be ones that allow you to make educated decisions.

DOCUMENT ALL CALLS AND/OR MEETINGS

Things get forgotten or slip through the cracks very easily. This is why documenting conversations matters: it allows you to go back and keep track of things that need to get done. It also helps you hold the property manager accountable. This goes back to things being traceable; you always want the ability to go back and look at past conversations and performance.

Every week, we document our conversations with our property management company on our weekly calls in a spreadsheet. We create separate tabs for each week so we can go back to the previous week and review all the notes then create new notes for the current week. Follow-up is so important in business. If you are not following up on previous discussions with your property management company, you will be surprised at how much is not getting done that you thought was.

PUT SYSTEMS IN PLACE

If you are a syndicator, you are managing other people's money, which means you better not be waiting for something to go wrong. You should instead be putting systems in place to always reduce or eliminate risk. As we mentioned in Chapter 1, always be proactive, not reactive. Do not wait for the property manager to tell you when something is not right; try to see and question things before they go wrong. Most managers, by default, are very reactive, which is why you need systems in place to help your team look to the future and be prepared.

Systems are also another way to separate yourself from your competition. Managing apartments is all about who puts out the most fires most efficiently and who reduces the number of fires they have; if you do this effectively, you will have a stronger business than your competitors. Systems help you achieve this; they weave proactivity into your day-to-day functioning. All this won't seem so important when things are going well, but it's when things start to go wrong that you will wish you put these measures in place in advance. Waiting for things to go wrong is a bad idea. Things will not always go according to plan, which is why being proactive is so important and allows you to recover much faster than others.

PROPERTY VISITS

You must visit your properties to check in on the property manager. If you do not, how will you really know what is going on with the renovations, projects, and overall condition of the property? We currently visit our properties every other week until the major work has been completed. Once the property is stabilized, we visit once per month—and we do not live in our market. Remember, the devil is in the details. If you are not there seeing it for yourself, you will not know the quality of the work being done. Pictures are not enough; they can be taken at deceptive angles or doctored.

We suggest walking *all* vacant units and units under renovation during every visit. You never know what you are going to find or what talking point will come up because of this. If your property management company knows you never visit the property, what incentive does it have to keep it in the shape you expect? Trust us when we say if you do not hold your property management company accountable, things will start to slip.

In addition to your planned visits, we recommend showing up at your property unannounced. If your property management company knows when you are coming, the property will look its best for your visit. You could be surprised to discover what goes on day to day if you show up unannounced. The goal of this exercise is to understand how the property looks, feels, and operates for your residents and potential residents when they are on the property. Here's what to look out for:

- What is the level of cleanliness and overall curb appeal of the property?
- Were reports about projects underway or completed accurate?
- How do the renovations look?
- Are things out of place?
- What is the staff doing upon your arrival?

Also, drive by the property at night to check:

- Do the gates work properly?
- Is it loud outside, or is there anyone causing a disturbance?
- Do the lights work, and are they adjusted properly?
- Does the property feel safe?
- Are there lights left on that should not be left on?

These are all things you cannot discover if you don't visit the property. Always trust your manager, but also verify that trust and check on your property. If you do not have boots on the ground, find someone who can go by the property from time to time to check on it. Do this even if you must hire someone. Your property management company should be handling these things, but the only way to ensure they are being done is to check on them from time to time and hold the company accountable.

WEEKLY CALLS WITH REPORTS

Are you having weekly calls with your property manager? If not, you should be! This is where you discuss current and upcoming projects, property performance, challenges, and KPIs. We suggest weekly calls because so much can change week over week, and as we have discussed, things can slip through the cracks very quickly. Once your property is stabilized, you can decide whether weekly is too much—remember, though, that what you manage gets done.

What reports are you receiving during the weekly calls? We receive a weekly comparison of:

- Budget
- Updated rent roll
- Updated project list
- Interior renovations update
- Snapshot of vacant units
- Notices to vacate
- Renovated units

We also receive a general weekly report that includes things like:

- Occupancy
- Preleased units
- Traffic counts and conversions
- Vacant units rented and not rented
- Move-ins and move-outs
- Ready units versus down units
- Delinquent counts and amount
- Promises to pay
- Lease expirations
- Work orders received and completed
- Month-to-date total income received
- Reasons for cancels
- Denials and move outs

This is in addition to any miscellaneous information, such as large repairs and suggestions. Suffice to say, you should be receiving a lot of information from your property management company in order to track the performance of your property.

ACCESS TO PROPERTY MANAGEMENT SOFTWARE

The weekly reports we mentioned above are typically based on data gathered by a property management software your management company uses. RealPage, Yardi, and ResMan are a few examples of such software. These weekly reports are only snapshots of your property's performance. For ideal monitoring, you should also have access to this software to view up-to-date and daily statistics. This allows you to look at the statistics mentioned in the weekly reports in more detail. It will help you dive deep into information on potential residents, lead sources, the work status of residents, lead pipelines, and so on. These statistics allow you to see trends and get a feel for the flow of traffic. Looking at a weekly report is great, but when you look at statistics day over day, you can identify more opportunities.

MONTHLY REPORTING

How detailed are your monthly reports? Are you only looking at the income statement, which is a summary of your monthly income and expenses? If this is all you are looking at or getting from your property manager, you are not digging deep enough—and quite possibly, you may have hired the wrong property management company. Our reports are 200-plus pages. They include each and every payment and expense along with proof of payments from our property management company, among many other things. Remember, this is a business, and you should be treating it as such. You want to monitor every dollar that goes in and out of your business and not be content with just a summary.

Here is the index page of our monthly report so you can see all the items included in the report we review.

Index

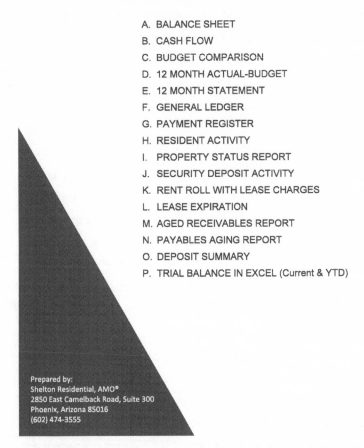

Prepared by:
Shelton Residential, AMO®
2850 East Camelback Road, Suite 300
Phoenix, Arizona 85016
(602) 474-3555

YEARLY BUDGETS

Do you give the property manager your yearly budget in advance, or do you have them create their own? Different operators do this differently, and there is no right or wrong way. However, for all our properties, we have two budgets: (1) our proforma per our investment summary, and (2) the property manager's budget. We have our property management company create its own budget first and then adjust based on their first run-through. In our experience, their budgets are much more aggressive than ours. If you show your hand too early, they may lower their expectations. So, let them tell you what they think the budget should be first.

One great example of how this worked in our favor is a property we own and operate in Phoenix, Arizona. The property management company provided a budget that was $225,000 higher in NOI than our budget. This meant if the property manager missed their budget by $225,000, we would still be flat to ours. But if you give the management company a lower budget, they will lower their expectations and work to that budget.

It is important to be on the same page with your property management company as far as your business plan goes, but that does not mean they have to see all your cards. People tend to play down to the level of their competition or expectations, and you want your property management company working for you at its highest level, so we prefer to have their budget be a stretch goal to reach for.

SECRET SHOPPER REPORTS

We secret shop/audit our properties monthly, and we do this in two ways. First, we have someone call into the property and speak with the staff or leave a message. Some of the things we are looking for on this call are:

- Did they answer, and if not, how long did it take them to call back?
- Were they friendly, inviting, and professional?
- Did they sell the benefits of the community?
- Did they ask for the close—i.e., did they schedule a visit or ask the person to fill out an application?

The next thing we do is set up a new email account and send the property an online inquiry. It is important to send these emails from a new email every month and change the message so it's not easy to identify. If the manager knows it is you, they are more likely to be on top of it. The goal here is to know how prospective residents are communicated with and treated. This will help you work with the property management team to improve its processes. Here are some items you should be looking for in the online shopper report.

- Did the leasing agent acknowledge and thank you for your inquiry?
- Did they answer any questions you asked, or did the email seem to be copied and pasted?

- Were there links to pictures/videos/floorplans of the property and nearby schools and attractions?
- How long did it take for the leasing agent to follow up?
- Did they ask for the close—i.e., did they schedule a visit or ask you to fill out an application?

First impressions are everything. By doing these seemingly simple checks and audits, you can separate yourself from your competition very quickly. Always think about how you can best treat your prospective residents and how you can add value to them even before they sign a lease. Visit www.bestinclassbook.co for our Secret Shopper Scorecard template.

CONCLUSION

Managing property managers may seem like a lot of work, and it is! However, you have a responsibility to your investors and your business to put processes in place that encourage the best and most efficient results. If you are overwhelmed, take things one step at a time. Not all of these measures need to be set up on day one for you to be successful. The best advice we can give is to lay out a plan in advance and take small steps toward executing it a little at a time. Many of these systems and processes were not set up when we purchased our first property. But little by little, we added them, and now we have a great system that allows us to be more efficient and get the best out of our property managers. And we will continue to add, tweak, and improve these systems as needs and markets change.

Also, be sure to recognize and celebrate your property manager on their wins. They are working their tails off for you and your investors, and you need to celebrate with your team along the way. Turnover is your biggest expense (whether that is a resident or an employee, it does not matter). If you treat your team with respect and as equal partners, you will have much better results in getting them to work with you on many of these items.

Lastly, even when your property performs ahead of plan for a given month or better than expected, this does not mean there are not opportunities to improve. You should always drill down, peel back the onion a layer further, and be proactive, even when things are seemingly going well. It is much more difficult to solve problems when things are not going according to plan; this is when people are stressed out, they make emotional decisions, or they force the issue. If you implement a plan to improve when things are going well, it is much easier to achieve. Just like they say, "Always be closing," you should also "Always be improving."

For a copy of our e-book, *Managing the Manager*, visit www. bestinclassbook.co.

CHAPTER 8

KEY PERFORMANCE INDICATORS (KPIs)

If you can't measure it, you can't manage it.

—PETER DRUCKER

KPIs are the backbone of any successful business. KPIs are measurable values that demonstrate how effectively a company is achieving its key business objectives. Organizations use KPIs at multiple levels to evaluate their success at reaching targets. KPIs should be used in every single business. As Asset Managers, you too should have specific KPIs to track and measure the trends and performance of your property.

You need to be able to look at how your properties are performing at a moment's notice. Data and information are power, and KPIs allow you to collect real-time data and information so you can make accurate decisions. Since KPIs help Asset Managers identify trends, these should be tracked and measured over time—not just week over week or month over month, but even year over year in some cases. By tracking these trends, you will be able to identify both lagging and leading indicators to help create better efficiencies and make better decisions for your properties. An example of lagging indicators would be tracking the trend of occupancy for the property, and an example of a leading indicator could be forecasting upcoming vacant units. Both are crucial to making the right decisions to drive and maintain NOI.

Managing apartments is all about putting out fires efficiently and reducing the number of fires as much as possible. KPIs allow you to identify potential issues and bottlenecks that may arise. In some cases, they also allow you to identify a problem *before* there is one. For example, consider the leading indicator mentioned above on forecasting future vacant units. If you can put a plan in place to turn these units instead of waiting to make a decision, you can save time, money, and stress for both you and your property management company!

We're sure you are asking yourself the same question we were when we first got started: "Shouldn't your property management company be tracking these things for you?"

Although some of the items we will get into later in this chapter are tracked by property management companies, the truth is most property management companies are not savvy enough to know how to utilize this data to help drive your business. This is why you need to take it upon yourself to track these things and harness this information. Remember, the success of your investment is your responsibility. It's up to you to provide yourself and your property management company with the best tools to succeed, and KPIs are undoubtedly one of those tools. Ultimately, KPIs will help your property manager with the execution of your business plan as well as allow you to track and hold them accountable in the areas that most impact your business and NOI.

We can sit here and bore you to death by talking about each and every KPI we measure and why, but we won't do that—mainly because that would be a book in and of itself! But we will cover some of our favorite KPIs in this chapter, how we track them, and what we do with that information. We have also provided a list of over fifty different KPIs we like to track, just in case you were wondering.

KPI 1: INCOME—RENT COLLECTIONS AND NOI

The very basic level of tracking KPIs is measuring and monitoring your income streams. This seems very obvious, but being able to track income as it ebbs and flows is necessary.

Often, this can get lost in the shuffle as you focus on all the other things going on with your property. Seeing a snapshot of income month over month and year over year gives you a starting point to identify potential challenges or opportunities—it can be invaluable.

KPI 2: AVERAGE RENT/UNIT TYPE AND LOSS TO LEASE

How are you tracking the execution of your business plan and ensuring it is actually producing the results you need? Average rent/unit type and loss to lease burn-off are key indicators of this.

Especially during the value-add phase, you want to keep track of where you are achieving your target rents and where you are not. If you have a property with multiple unit types and sizes, this can be hard to track without a system in place, so make sure you implement one. Tracking this metric allows you to adjust your business plan according to accurate data instead of just guessing or hoping.

Loss to lease burn-off may seem simple to calculate, but operating an apartment building is a very fluid process with things changing daily. Seeing where you stand in this category puts you in touch with the actual progress you are making. If you are not burning off as much loss to lease as you anticipated, you may need to adjust your rents, change your interior renovation package to increase demand, or adjust your marketing strategy.

KPI 3: WORK ORDERS

There are many opportunities for tracking work orders. We like to track current open and closed work orders for multiple categories (HVAC, appliances, electrical, plumbing, roof, general maintenance, etc.). By doing this, we are able to see things like the average time for completion of each category, the number of open versus closed work orders each week, and the category that is being called on for repair most frequently. Using this data, here are some questions you will want to ask yourself:

- Is the team getting to these work orders quickly enough?
- Do you have a bigger issue you can fix now to reduce the number of calls for this specific category?

By reducing the time spent on work orders, you are freeing up time for your maintenance staff to do other things to improve the property and reducing your month-to-month expenses.

KPI 4: LASAL—LEADS, APPOINTMENTS, SHOWINGS, APPLICATIONS, LEASES

We learned this KPI from our friend and mentor Neal Bawa.

For this KPI, we don't just measure leads and conversion to leases, we measure leads, appointments, showings, applications, and leases separately. Not only do you want to know the sources of your leads and how many of each of these you are getting on a daily, weekly, and monthly basis, you also want to track the conversion of each into the next step so you can identify bottlenecks and what needs improvement.

Imagine only knowing you had forty-five leads last week and one lease signed. In this scenario, it is difficult to really know what the issue is other than the conversion percentage was low. But what if you knew that of those forty-five leads, there were four appointments booked? Of those four appointments, there were three showings, and of those showings, there was one application, and that one application led to one lease? Now you know that somewhere between the leads and appointments, there is something creating a low conversion rate. Maybe the leads are not quality leads, or the property management company is not getting to those leads quickly enough. Regardless, you have identified a bottleneck, and you can dig in further to investigate what's happening instead of just guessing. We have our manager provide us an update on this KPI weekly (see the example below). We track this week over week and month over month.

LASAL	WEEKLY GOAL	%	ACTUAL	%
Leads	40		40	
Appointments	10	25%	6	13%
Showings	8	80%	4	67%
Applications	4	50%	2	50%
Leases	2	50%	1	50%

KPI 5: PROSPECT TO TENANT CONVERSIONS

If you can't measure which avenue of your marketing is working, how will you know where to put more energy? This directly ties into LASAL and trying to identify the bottlenecks in your marketing and leasing efforts.

The goal behind this KPI is tracking where most of your leads are coming from, what percentage you are converting into actual leases, and which sources give you the best bang for your buck. If you are not tracking where you are getting the majority of your conversions, you are likely spending money on sources that are not getting you your highest return on investment.

We believe effective marketing is market and neighborhood specific, so things like RentLinx or Apartments.com may be great tools in one market but not in others. You may have one property with great visibility and access to a high-traffic street where you don't need much paid marketing and another that is not on a main road and has limited visibility and thus may need more marketing than usual. When it comes to marketing, leads are important, but the quality of those leads and the conversions are really what you want to track.

GENERAL LIST OF KPIs

Here is a list of all the KPIs we currently track using various software tools. Some are tracked daily, weekly, or monthly; they may provide a current snapshot of performance or go back twelve months to identify and track trends. These KPIs are tracked for each of our properties individually, as well as for all properties combined so we can track the performance of the whole portfolio. You can also get this list at www.bestinclassbook.co.

- Total Units
- Total Square Feet
- Average Rent
- Rent per Square Foot
- Average Market Rent
- Leased Units
- Market Potential $
- Current Potential $
- Percent to Market (Leased)
- Loss to Lease
- Preleased
- Turnover

- Vacant Ready
- Physical Occupancy Overall
- Given Notice
- In Eviction
- Rent Collections Month to Date
- Rent Collections Month over Month
- Upcoming Move-Ins
- Evictions
- Upcoming Move-Outs
- Turnover Units
- Month-to-Month Leases
- Historical Physical Occupancy
- Skips
- Market Rent Summary by Unit (Potential versus Actual)
- Upcoming Lease Expirations
- Leases Signed Month over Month
- Prospect Sources Current Month
- Prospect Traffic Current Month
- Overall Prospect Sources
- Overall Prospect-to-Tenant Conversions
- LASAL Conversions
- Days Vacant per Unit
- Turnover Availability Forecast (Completion and Number of Units)
- Overdue Turnover Details
- Turnover Details
- Open Work Orders by Category
- Closed Work Orders Current Month by Category

- Closed Work Orders by Category
- Rehab Tasks
- Rehab-under-Bid Tasks (Budget versus Actual)
- Rehab-in-Progress Tasks (Budget versus Actual)
- Total Income Month to Date
- Total Income Month over Month
- Total Expenses Month to Date
- Total Expenses Month over Month
- Individual Expenses Accounts Month to Date
- Individual Expenses Accounts Month over Month
- Cash Flow Month over Month
- Break-Even Analysis (Occupancy and Income)
- NOI Month to Date
- NOI Month over Month

CONCLUSION

Go to www.bestinclassbook.co to see some examples of how these KPIs look when the data is populated into graphs and charts. As you will see, it makes decision making much more efficient and it is easier to see what is working—as well as identify areas of opportunity—when you use KPIs and data the right way. Imagine getting a daily snapshot of your property's performance. Don't you think you'll be able to make better decisions quicker? We sure do! It will also save you money, as it will identify where you get the best bang for your buck on things like marketing dollars by evaluating those specific KPIs.

Creating KPIs and tracking them can be overwhelming, but they don't have to be. There are tools and companies that can help you get this set up for relatively cheap. If your property management company cannot provide a business intelligence dashboard from its property management software, there are companies out there with integrations that can take your data and place it into its software to create these dashboards and KPIs for you. Or you can hire a developer on Upwork to create your own. Technology will be the differentiator for Asset Managers over the next five to ten years and can quickly separate you from your competition or leave you in the dust.

Ultimately, what you measure is what you can manage. KPIs allow you to be proactive and peek into the future by using past trends to make educated decisions. You will be a better investor and operator when you use KPIs to help you make your business decisions. It's about never-ending and constant improvement, and KPIs make this a much easier process.

CHAPTER 9

MARKETING

Marketing without data is like driving with your eyes closed.

—DAN ZARRELLA

The majority of Asset Managers, owners, and operators leave marketing to their property management companies to oversee. Less than 1 percent actually do any marketing on their own. If you are in the 99 percent, you should consider going against the grain and not solely relying on your management company to promote and market your properties. There is just too much variability in the quality of marketing between property managers, and you never know what you are going to get. As an Asset Manager, you want to have your own marketing channels to rely on just in case things are not going according to plan. We believe this is extremely important and can take the performance of your property to the next level.

Almost all the profit in the apartment industry is between the 87 percent and 97 percent mark. That's where the overwhelming majority of your profit lies, if not all your profit. So when your occupancy reduces 1 percent, your profit is often reduced by up to 10 percent. But for most managers, all they see is that their occupancy dropped only 1 percent, and they don't react. That's a problem. Even if your marketing efforts can help increase the economic occupancy just 1 to 2 percent, your profits will skyrocket with that. Focusing on the details is important, and this is one detail that is often overlooked.

In this chapter, we'll explore basic marketing housekeeping and what you need to keep in mind if venturing into this territory for the first time.

ADVERTISING

When overseeing marketing, the first thing you'll want to do is make sure all your current marketing by the property management company is up to date, professional, and presents well. Sometimes, you have just seconds to catch the eye of your potential resident before they move on to the next listing, so you need to make sure all your marketing channels have updated and professional photos of the property, a video walkthrough, an interesting description, and all the details about the property. As you renovate your property, be sure to update all your marketing platforms with that information as well. Do not rely on the property management company to get this done; go through the listings with a fine-toothed comb.

Check out your competition and see how their listings look to get an idea of what you want on yours. Below are two examples to show you the difference between a detailed, professional listing and one that needs more work. We have stricken out the names of these properties in the description to keep them anonymous.

EXAMPLE 1

About our Apartments

A PERSONAL OASIS IN ONE OF PHOENIX'S MOST DESIRED NEIGHBORHOODS

Discover an engaging, energizing, and harmonious life at our apartments. Located in the Uptown Phoenix neighborhood, we offer easy access to some of the area's newest restaurants, bars, farmers' markets, and more. Our location close to the light rail means your daily commute could be car free, allowing you to trade traffic for quick rides. Spend weekends exploring and absorbing the community around you, then come home to a relaxing space full of inviting amenities and convenient resident services designed with your comfort in mind.

MORE THAN AN APARTMENT, OUR APARTMENT IS A LIFESTYLE

Enjoy the unique characteristics of Phoenix's newest neighborhood, Uptown. With local-favorite hang outs and chic eateries just steps from your door, our apartments in Uptown Phoenix are the perfect places to call home, make new friends, and experience an upscale desert lifestyle. Our pet-friendly apartment community offers thoughtfully curated, twenty-four-hour amenity spaces, including an expansive sky deck overlooking Camelback Mountain and Piestewa Peak, luxe resident lounge, ultra-luxe pool, bike shop, solopreneur workspaces, resident services, and more.

EXPLORE ALL THAT UPTOWN PHOENIX HAS TO OFFER

Uptown Phoenix provides the perfect backdrop for our apartments. With easy access to the light rail and our unique Central Valley location, residents can explore some of Phoenix's best and most notable restaurants, shops, attractions, and nightlife car free.

Apartment Amenities

Unique Features

Amenities Vary By Unit

- Twenty-four-hour package lockers
- Accent pendant lighting over kitchen islands
- Celebrity VIP parking
- Chef-inspired community kitchen

- Conference room and cyber café
- Electronic entry locks
- Full-size in-unit washers and dryers
- Luxury penthouse homes
- Modern grey cabinets
- Luxury apartment homes
- Oversized quartz countertops and islands
- Pet utopia, featuring dog wash and fenced dog run
- Private balconies
- Private rooftop patios
- Refrigerators with bottom-mount freezers
- Spacious walk-in closets with built-in shelving
- Stainless-steel appliances
- Ultra-luxe pool and spa with towel service
- Wine chillers
- Wood-style plank flooring

Pet Policy

Dogs Allowed

- Ninety-pound weight limit
- Two-pet limit

Cats Allowed

- Two-pet limit

Parking

Surface lot, covered, and other
Garage: $10

Property Information

- Built in 2018
- 237 units/four stories

Lease Lengths

- Six-, seven-, eight-, nine-, ten-, eleven-, and twelve-month leases available

Services

- Wi-Fi at pool and clubhouse
- Daycare
- Maintenance on site
- Doorman
- Twenty-four-hour availability
- Trash pickup—door to door
- Online services
- Planned social activities
- Health-club discount
- Guest apartment
- Pet play area
- Pet washing station
- Public transportation
- Key-fob entry

Interior

- Elevator
- Business center
- Clubhouse

- Lounge
- Multi-use room
- Breakfast/coffee concierge
- Storage space
- Disposal chutes

Outdoor Space

- Gated
- Courtyard
- Grill
- Picnic area
- Balcony

Fitness and Recreation

- Fitness center
- Spa
- Pool
- Bike storage
- Basketball court
- Media center/movie theatre

Features

- High-speed internet access
- Washer/dryer—in unit
- Air conditioning
- Heating
- Ceiling fans
- Smoke free

- Cable ready
- Storage units
- Double vanities
- Tub/shower
- Wheelchair accessible (rooms)

Kitchen

- Dishwasher
- Garbage disposal
- Ice maker
- Stainless-steel appliances
- Island kitchen
- Microwave
- Oven
- Range
- Refrigerator
- Freezer

Living Space

- Hardwood floors
- Carpet
- Vinyl flooring
- Vaulted ceilings
- Views
- Walk-in closets
- Linen closets
- Window coverings
- Large bedrooms

Security

- Package service
- Property manager on site
- Concierge

EXAMPLE 2

About our Apartments

At our apartments in Phoenix, experience great living. The convenient setting in the 85006 area of Phoenix is a popular place to live. Make sure to check out the apartment floorplan options. This community has a unique selection of amenities and features, like smoke-free options and high-speed internet access. Stop by to talk about leasing your new apartment.

Apartment Amenities

Parking

- Surface lot
- One space

Property Information

- Built in 2001
- 215 units/two stories

Services

- Laundry facilities

Features

- High-speed internet access
- Air conditioning
- Smoke free

Now, these are extreme examples, and they are not comparable properties, but as you can see, there is a huge difference here. Example 1 paints the picture of the area, the community, the lifestyle, all of its benefits, and why you would want to live there, while Example 2 just lists the bare minimum. How you present your property online will have dramatic effects on your results.

SIGNAGE

Your signage is also crucial when it comes to marketing. Walk-in and drive-through traffic are just as important as online traffic. You could even argue they're more important. If you can get a person to walk in or call the property and speak to someone in person, your chance of closing them is much higher than just having that person fill out one of the hundreds of online requests for more information. This is why signage matters so much. Always make sure it is in the best possible shape. Is it visible as people drive by? Is it well lit at night? Are there areas that get heavy traffic where you can add things like banners, flags, and bandit signs?

With regard to walk-in traffic and noticeable signage, it's also important your leasing office is easy to find, welcoming, and fully stocked with all promotional items (e.g., rent pricing sheets, floorplan layouts, flyers, etc.). First impressions are extremely important, and you'll want to take advantage of this.

PLATFORMS AND TOOLS

Is your property management company utilizing all the platforms and tools out there? Tools such as Zumper are often used when your property is advertised on a large majority of platforms. Notice, we said "majority" and not "all." This means there are still several platforms out there you are not using that you can and should be taking advantage of. The more visibility your property has, the better chance you have of driving more traffic, so you want to be on as many channels as possible. You'll also want to do some research on local platforms that may not be as well known as the major platforms like Apartments.com and Apartment Guide. Do not make the mistake of only trusting the most well-known platforms, as you may be missing out on an opportunity. Some of the smaller platforms are market specific and perform better in certain markets.

Did you know you can list multiple units on many of the online marketing platforms? Well, you can! So instead of just listing your property once, you can list units 1A, 2A,

3A, etc., and post up to fifty-plus listings on some of these platforms. The reason you want to do this is because your property will get more exposure than just having one listing that will get buried under hundreds of other competitors.

A lot of these platforms will also allow you to refresh your listings. Often, you'll put your listing on a platform, and then in an hour, somebody else will put their listing on the same platform, and now, theirs is on top. Your listing gets buried within a couple hours, and no one sees your listing once it is buried. The process of refreshing your listings is a very key process, and we try and do as much of it as possible. For example, on RentLinx, we refresh up to four times a day. And that bumps our listing back up to the top of the list of results.

Local businesses are also a great way to establish close relationships and market your property. Having some sort of referral program or cross-marketing plan with local businesses, such as schools, hospitals, shopping centers, and corporations, should be on your list of platforms and ways to market.

We also use Facebook Marketplace. Facebook Marketplace is the hardest to use compared to all the other platforms because it is an active conversation. If you just list something on Marketplace, you will see a very large number of people with the same exact question, which is "Is this available?" You're going to see that over and over again. It requires a back-and-forth conversation, which is very manpower heavy. However, we have seen good results using Facebook Marketplace, and we highly suggest you encourage your property management company to utilize this tool to promote your properties.

CONCLUSION

Great marketing is the process of generating a large number of resident leads or prospective resident leads by actively engaging residents and posting a large number of listings across the market. We make sure we have listings on lots of different platforms, like Craigslist, GoSection8, Rentler, Zillow Marketplace, RentLinx, Zumper, Apartments.com, Apartment Guide, and Facebook Marketplace. This takes work, and it is not something you can exactly operate on autopilot. But it's something that should be considered in your business model. If you have a virtual assistant, this would be a great task for them to be responsible for. Once you have marketing systems and processes in place, the key is to track the results using data and trends to figure out where you are getting the best bang for your buck and which platforms perform better than others.

CHAPTER 10

LEASING

Efficiency is doing better what is already being done.

—PETER DRUCKER

Leasing is the foundation of the multifamily industry and the lifeline of your asset. Everything flows from it, and if your leasing is great, mostly everything else will fall into place. As they say, revenue cures all. With leasing, much like with marketing, it is best not to rely only on the property management company. You should be involved and help shape the processes and procedures behind your leasing strategies. There are too many things to consider when it comes to leasing and its many moving parts, so having a team develop and execute the plan is critical (this includes your property management company as well as your internal team). Leaving these types of decisions to the leasing agent is not recommended and will end with less positive results.

This chapter will cover some of the most important points you must keep in mind when it comes to leasing, tools that can help you improve returns, and much more.

LEASING: THE BASICS

There is a lot at play when it comes to leasing.

- Highest rent versus occupancy
- Current market rents versus renovated market rents
- Lease expirations per month
- Timing for in-house turns versus full renovation
- Performance compared to budget

These are just to name a few. In our opinion, the key to leasing is the team behind the leasing. A big part of that is the quality of your leasing agent. What is their personality like? Are they friendly and outgoing? Are they asking for the sale—meaning, are they trying to sell the potential resident on all the benefits of the community and close them? This is a sales position, so you want someone with sales experience who is very personable. If they are not, you may have the wrong person. As we discussed in Chapter 2 on building a team, placing the right type of person in a position is just as important as the strategies and procedures you have in place. If you have the wrong person in a position, you are setting them and yourself up to fail from the start. Take your time when hiring a leasing agent, and make sure they have the personality, traits, and qualifications of someone that will sell your community.

Just as important as your leasing agent is having the right manager in place to help that leasing agent execute the leasing strategy and hold them accountable. This position requires a much stronger skillset, as they will need both managerial and sales experience. If your manager doesn't know how to sell, how can they hold someone accountable whose job it is to sell? Again, take your time when hiring for both positions, as they are going to be the ones on the property day in and day out, driving your asset. This is a people business, and you need to hire the right team that will focus on the people (i.e., your current and future residents).

Once you have the right leasing team in place, it is time to dig into your processes and procedures to make sure you and your property management company are doing everything to convert those leads into leases. As we have mentioned in other chapters in this book, if you don't measure it, you can't manage it. So, you will need a system in place to track conversions and identify bottlenecks so you can get the best results for your efforts. Which leads us back to LASAL.

LASAL (LEADS, APPOINTMENTS, SHOWINGS, APPLICATIONS, LEASES)

We have already covered LASAL in the chapter on KPIs (Chapter 8), but it is so important, we will mention it again here. You need to track your conversion ratios so you can constantly improve your leasing operations. Leasing is not about doing one thing right; it is about creating an efficient system that has checks and balances to eventually become a well-oiled machine. For reference, we have included our LASAL Calculator at www.bestinclassbook.co.

Along the lines of LASAL, there are other systems and processes you should ensure your leasing agent is following; these will help you get the best results. One of these is the timeliness of responses to all inquiries. If you are not calling a lead back the same day and, quite honestly, within the half-hour, you're wasting your time. It is highly likely a potential resident is not only inquiring about an apartment at your property, which means they are shopping several other properties as well. Whoever calls them back first and maybe second is going to get the appointment.

LIFO (LAST IN, FIRST OUT)

The restaurant industry has a term called FIFO, which stands for "first in, first out." This means the food being stored is used in the order it was received: the first in gets used first. This system allows for less waste and more efficient storage. We use a system called LIFO, which stands for "last in, first out" and means the lead that just came in is the one that will receive an immediate call back. This is because we find internet leads are gold in the first five minutes, silver in the next hour, and bronze for the rest of the day. If you are calling your leads the following day, they are stale and will likely not produce many results. This is too important a part of your business to outsource, and you should watch it carefully.

For sponsors or companies with many properties, you may consider having a call center that covers your entire portfolio for most of the day (7:00 a.m. to 7:00 p.m.). Firms can use this call center to take the initial phone calls and attempt to schedule an appointment with the leasing agent. The person answering the call will have access to the leasing agent's calendar, updated daily, to allow them to book the appointment directly. This relieves a lot of pressure at the property level so the leasing agent can be focused on closing the higher-probability leads instead of juggling everything on their own. This is a high-cost process but well worth it if you are at that scale. Again, this is for larger players with many properties.

LEASE RENT OPTIMIZER SYSTEMS

Your property management company should also be keeping a very close eye on your existing market rents and how those compare to your competition. Some companies use a lease rent optimizer (LRO) system. This system helps property management companies forecast and analyze market demand and unit availability as well as set unit pricing based on dynamically measured consumer demand. If you do not use an LRO system, keeping an eye on average rents per unit and your competition will be key. Either way, you need to know what the market is charging to stay on top of your rents, which will ultimately affect the number of lease-ups you are closing each month. The leasing agent is important, but they cannot do much if your rents are set too high.

MANAGING FLOW

It is also smart to have a plan for how many units should be vacant at one time to manage flow. This not only means you want to keep an eye on notices to vacate and evictions (which ultimately leads to vacant units), but it also means you want to make sure you stagger your leases. Essentially, you do not want a large percentage of your leases to expire in one month. In a perfect world, you would take the number of units and divide those by twelve, and that would be the number of leases that expire every month. This way, you do not have huge ups and downs with occupancy. If you do have these large swings, it may force you to be less aggressive on your renewal increases, and that, obviously, affects your NOI. This is why you will often see properties that offer not only twelve-month leases but also ten-, eleven-, and thirteen-month leases in order to stagger them a bit. Depending on the market you are investing in, you may want to stagger more in the spring and summer versus the fall and winter if lease-ups drop drastically based on weather. Staggering your leases will allow for more consistent occupancy and help your leasing agent.

Another item your leasing agent should be aware of to help manage flow is the timing of in-house turns versus a full renovation. Typically, this is where you, as an Asset Manager, will need to be involved to help communicate the number of vacant units you are willing to have at a given time. If a full renovation takes three weeks and an in-house turn takes just three days, this is a huge difference. If you have several vacant units coming up, you may decide to fully renovate just a percentage of them and do in-house turns on the others to keep the occupancy up.

When we're looking at leasing, we want to be about 95 percent occupied on our properties. Otherwise, you may not be charging enough for rents, which means you are not maximizing your profits. There will be times, however, when it may make sense to be higher than 95 percent—maybe there is a crisis happening or you are selling the property. In these cases, you may want 100 percent occupancy. But more often than not, you will want to be testing the market and pushing your rents to drive NOI. An occupancy of 100 percent is not always a positive thing; it's possible your rents are too low, so you should test them to find out.

Renewing leases is just as important (if not more so) than securing new leases. Turnover is your biggest expense, and anything you can do to renew leases is worth looking into (as long as the renewed leases are at the rates you need to execute your business plan). Your leasing agent should have a process in place where they reach out to residents well in advance to renew their leases, at least sixty to ninety days out. This allows enough time for communication with the resident as well as getting notice far enough in advance if the resident does not want to renew their lease. Since turnover is your biggest expense, you may want to implement some creative ways to encourage your residents to stay. Obviously, this should be happening by providing a sense of community the entire time they live at the property, but it also pays to do other things that may get residents to stay. One thing we have done in the past that has worked out well is sending an anniversary letter/card congratulating the resident on their long residency instead of sending a renewal letter. This gives them that sense of community and belonging versus just another person paying the property money. Doing creative things like this can go a long way when it comes to resident retention and lease renewals.

TRACKING

I know we sound like a broken record, but it is important to continue to track and measure results so you can continue to identify bottlenecks. Leasing is no exception and in fact, should be one of your top priorities. Taking your foot off the gas or becoming complacent is a recipe for disaster. So, even when things are going well, are you completing monthly shopper reports on the leasing staff as mentioned in Chapter 7 (Managing the Manager) for quality control and potential resident experience? Are you following up with the property management company on those reports? If not, you need to be. Remember, be proactive, not reactive!

When tracking these types of things, it is always best to track over a longer period of time and not just week over week. We suggest going back two to three months at a minimum to be able to get real measured results. There is no excuse to be flying blind nowadays. Today more than ever, you have the ability—or you should have the ability—to have data in the palm of your hands. It is a matter of just reading it and making sense of it. That's what we do every day.

CONCLUSION

Many of the decisions you will need to make that are covered in this chapter will come down to how the property is performing compared to your budget. Ultimately, it boils down to where you are in your business plan. Every business plan ebbs and flows, and there is no one decision that is right for every situation. This is why you need to be involved in each decision; you need to be leading the charge. One month or year, you may want to push market rents higher; the next, you may only want to focus on occupancy. Things change and so do your plan and execution. Work together with your leasing team to make the best decisions for the property at that given time.

CHAPTER 11

RENOVATION MANAGEMENT

Success is where preparation and opportunity meet.

—BOBBY UNSER

Renovation management is one of the main areas you tackle when you are doing a value-add play. You begin work on this while you are in escrow, making sure the rehab team, the property management team, and you (the Asset Manager) are on the same page regarding the level of rehab, the money you have allocated for capex, and the rents you are projecting to get. This is when you dial in all the details and ensure everyone is aligned in order to execute the business plan.

When it comes to renovation management, we like to hit

the ground running. If you need any permits, while you are in escrow would be a good time to start. You may need them if you are adding units, changing signage, adding certain amenities, or performing other construction work. Every city is different when it comes to permits, so make sure to check with your contractor. The reason we start working on permits while we are in escrow is it can take a significant amount of time to get all the permits, and we want to compress the renovation timeline as much as possible.

During this escrow time, also get multiple bids for the work that needs to be completed, and get recommendations for contractors from others. The lowest bid is not always the best and could cost you more money in the long run if they do shoddy work. Make sure to vet the contractor and check out their work prior to hiring them.

Once you have your permits and contractors in place, you're ready to begin the renovation work. We'll touch on the important things you need to keep in mind, outline strategies that have worked for us, and suggest some great tools that can help you on your journey.

CURB APPEAL AND DEFERRED MAINTENANCE

We always like to start with curb appeal and deferred maintenance so current residents see the changes. This makes them more willing to stay and pay higher rents, as they know new ownership is making the property a better, safer place to live. We have been successful with this strategy, and it cuts down on the cost of turnover, which can be significant.

Curb appeal can include well-lit signage, landscaping, exterior paint, and even asphalt repairs. Those things go a long way in making residents feel proud of the community they live in and offering a great first impression for potential renters. For one of our properties, we almost drove past it many times until we cleaned up the landscaping and improved the signage in the front. Now, you can see the property from afar, and our walk-in traffic drastically improved because the thousands of people that drive by it each day see how much nicer it is.

Fixing deferred maintenance issues will save you money in the long run. Review the report from your property inspection that tells you what is in most need of repair and where you can get the most bang for your buck. This could be a big boost to your NOI and have a tremendous domino effect. Say you fix something like leaks that haven't been addressed. Not only does this save you on the day-to-day expenses—which increases NOI—but it also results in fewer work orders from the residents. This frees up time for your maintenance staff to focus on other things and keeps the residents happy because they don't have to worry about calling to have something fixed as often.

Also, current residents are more likely to refer friends when they see money being put into the property. If you can get this work done, or at least started, prior to starting to raise rents, there is a much larger probability of current residents staying. You have to give them an incentive to stay, and you do that by putting money back into the property, making it more appealing and a safer place to live. Just raising the rents will likely result in many of the residents leaving.

TRACKING

It's important you track all the rehab projects in terms of timeliness and budget. Things can veer off course quickly if you are not paying attention, and you cannot rely on your contractor or property manager to do this for you. Things always take longer than planned, so it is your job to find out where the bottlenecks are. Tracking also includes checking out the work being done. There are times when someone might say something is finished, but it may not be completed or done to your liking. It's therefore crucial to check it out yourself, as pictures don't always tell the full story.

You can use software like Asana, Trello, Slack, Google Sheets, or even Excel to keep track of projects. You don't need to spend a lot of money, and you want to use a tool that everyone will be familiar with. Oftentimes, your collaborators are going to want to use something basic. Don't fight them on this; make the process easy for them to use.

You'll want to track each project based on a number of factors. Here are a few we track:

- Lead time needed to start
- How long it will take to complete
- Actual complete time
- Budget versus actual cost
- Completions per month
- Average completions per month over every three months for interiors

If you wait until the end of a projected finish date to check on a project, you may be disappointed. Make sure you clearly lay out expectations ahead of time. The bigger the project, the more you will need to stay on top of it to ensure you get the results you want. If things are not on schedule or budget, you will need to intervene and find out why. Things won't magically get better if you don't take action.

As far as tracking unit renovations, you will need to break them down per unit into as much detail as possible. When does the unit become vacant to begin work? What work will be completed? When is the estimated completion date? If you did not hit your completion date, why not? Over time, you will start to see trends or bottlenecks, and it is your job to address those issues so your renovation plan can become a finely tuned machine.

Here's a link to our renovation tracker: www.bestinclass-book.co. Note that it does not cover everything, nor does it work for every asset. We worked hard putting together something that works for the majority of properties, but feel free to use what we have and adjust it to fit your individual needs.

INTERIOR RENOVATIONS

If you have a small apartment building, your maintenance person can usually do some minor turns for units. But if you are doing a lot of work, you will need a team to execute renovations. You could use your third-party property management company, if you have one and they have a renovation team. Otherwise, you can hire an outside contractor. Regardless of who you use, you must check their work, particularly in the beginning, so the expectations are clearly laid out and you can adjust anything you do not like.

We want to reiterate it is crucial to set clear expectations ahead of time and make sure you understand how long a turn will take and how many can be done at any one time. It may take a couple units to build up steam on a big project. Many times, contractors will say a project will take less time than it will and they can do more units than they actually can deliver. Get everything in writing. Ensure there is proper lead time for anything that needs to be ordered ahead of time, like appliances, so you are not waiting on them. Make sure you get a detailed breakdown of costs for each item. You'll want to sign off on work being completed that matches the cost and scope before whoever did the work gets paid.

After you have finished a couple units at the renovation level of your business plan, review if you are getting the rent you projected. If you are getting more than what you hoped for, great. If you are getting less, you need to figure out why. It could be you have not finished your exterior improvements or added necessary amenities. Maybe the market has softened or your level of renovation is not good enough. Perhaps your competitors are doing something different than your renovations. Keep testing, and do more analysis until you find the maximum result.

You'll need to work with your property and regional managers to gain feedback on the renovations. They are helping to lease the units, so you need their input.

We have found the bulk of the work gets done in a timely manner, but the remaining few items on a unit can linger. You need to convey a sense of urgency so you can get a unit completed and rented. Let's say you have fifty-two units to renovate, and you can trim one week off of the renovation timeline. If you rent each unit for $1,000, you would have $12,000 in extra NOI. If you take that number and divide by a 6 cap, you just created $200,000 in value! Small adjustments can make a huge difference.

PIVOTING

Having a plan is important. It gives you direction and a blueprint to follow. However, a renovation plan does not have to be written in stone. We have pivoted our renovation plan a couple times. At one of our properties, we dialed back the interior renovations because we decided, along with our third-party property management team, that we didn't need to add a backsplash and six-panel doors to get the target rents. What we did want to do was spruce up the look of the property so we could push rents with a nicer exterior and be more competitive with the comps.

For this project, we worked with a designer to come up with a look that was modern and would add curb appeal. We will invest a good amount of money to paint the whole property but feel this pivot will push the NOI higher than we originally projected. Obviously, it's important to be well capitalized so you have options. You don't want to be using cash flow to fund your renovations and be limited in what you can do. Having multiple exit strategies and the money to finance your renovations gives you tremendous flexibility.

If you can get the rents you projected for a less ambitious renovation plan, consider going down that path. You do not want to over-improve your property if the submarket can't afford it or is not willing to pay for it. Keep checking in on the comps too, not just when you are looking to buy.

BUYING IN BULK

You can buy direct from China if you're purchasing a lot of product. "A lot" is a bit vague, but each item is different. We use a large property management company, so we've had the benefit of significant buying power. We've been able to get granite counters for basically the same price as Formica. We've also bought flooring in bulk, as we knew we needed a lot of it and could take advantage of a steep discount. You can rent a trailer if you have enough parking spots for all the items or use a unit if you are early in your renovation phase and are turning over many units each month. A lot depends on your individual property.

Some Asset Managers buy flooring, light fixtures, sinks, and other fittings in bulk to use across all their assets. They like having the necessary products on hand, as well as the discount they receive. Do not be afraid to push back on the prices of some items, as you never know when you'll be able to get a better deal. It can happen, though it often feels like magic when it does.

LENDER HOLDBACK

Lenders typically have an IRL that requires you to repair certain things first, as we have mentioned prior. They will give you a timeline and hold back money until these items are complete. The items are typically based on safety compliance, such as fixing railings or making an entrance-way handicap compliant. Make sure these repairs are all planned out with a margin for error to get them completed in time. Your lender will usually work with you if a project gets delayed or it makes sense to wait—for example, if the deadline for doing some pool repairs is August and you want to wait until summer is over so your residents can enjoy the pool—but you have to be proactive and talk to the lender ahead of time.

Lenders will typically over-budget for these items, so it is in your best interest to take care of the list and unlock the holdback to get reimbursed for the money sitting in escrow. The property management company we work with has an in-house general contractor that manages this for us, but not all property management companies offer this. If you don't have someone overseeing these items, you will need to keep track and make sure the work is done according to the lender's requirements. When each project is finished, the lender will send someone to inspect, sign off, and return the holdback funds. Sometimes, it takes months to get the money back from the lender, so be diligent about this, and make sure you keep in constant communication with the lender. The lender also has their list for how the reserves are spent over the life of the hold, which is separate from the IRL, but the reimbursement works the same.

RESIDENTS

You want to make sure your renovation plan limits the amount of time you have to disturb the residents. We made this mistake when we switched out sliding doors at one of our apartment buildings. We installed new doors with window panels, but we didn't properly account for how to cover the window openings for privacy. So we had to go back in and disturb the residents again. Painting and railings were being done at separate times as well, so the impact was one after the other. Sometimes, timing does not work in your favor, but you do your best. You may say it's not that big of a deal, and in the big picture, it is not. But to a resident, this unit is their home, and they do not want strangers in it or to be continuously disturbed.

It is also important to get residents' feedback before and during the renovations. They'll tell you what they really need and what will work. They may not like the commotion during the renovation, but we have received many thank-yous after the work is done, which is an amazing feeling. We are trying to improve communities and provide our residents with a place where they can feel proud to live. If you can do that, you are well on your way to becoming an excellent Asset Manager—and your NOI will surely increase too!

CONCLUSION

Remember, renovation management requires all team members to know the business plan, meticulous tracking, and frequent testing. If you can compress timelines and maximize efficiency, you will greatly increase the value of your property!

CHAPTER 12

VALUE-ADD STRATEGY

Strive for continuous improvement, instead of perfection.

—KIM COLLINS

A value-add strategy is one where there's typically in-place cash flow, but you're planning to increase that cash flow over time by making improvements, reducing expenses, improving operations, and/or repositioning the property. There really should be some element of value-add to every property you buy, even if it is a core or core-plus property. The more ways you can add value, the greater the return you can get when you eventually sell.

A value-add strategy brings you higher returns than other, more stabilized strategies because, in theory, there is higher reward for a higher risk. However, the risk is muted in multifamily if you have the right team in place that do their homework. This is not a guessing game; we use real data with elements of trial and error to execute a value-add strategy. This is forcing appreciation instead of hoping for it, as we control these elements.

In this chapter, we'll explore a few of the elements of a value-add strategy. The components of your strategy will, of course, depend on your property and its problems. Every facet of operation should have been studied during your underwriting and due diligence to determine the inefficiencies you can take advantage of. Once you have this list of what can be improved to add value, it's important to prioritize. You cannot tackle every single inefficiency right out of the gate, as you and your team need to be focused to execute properly. But one of the first areas you should tackle is branding.

BRANDING/REBRANDING

Rebranding is a great way to separate yourself from a previous bad owner. If you are doing a big value-add play, rebranding can help you separate the property from a previous image. It may have a bad reputation or reviews, or perhaps you need to re-tenant the property. Either way, rebranding helps. Rebranding is not a must, but it is one of the opportunities you may want to consider taking advantage of.

One of our properties was called Townhouse East when we purchased it. The property did not have townhouses nor did it look like one in any way. It was also not on the east side. Obviously, the name didn't convey the proper messaging at all. We changed the name to the hipper Midtown on 2nd. It may seem silly that a name change can help drive up NOI, but you'll be surprised at how all the different elements play a role. We also changed the signage and added the logo to two street-facing walls. Not only did this add some color to the blank walls, but it also gave us a lot of advertising for a relatively low cost.

At another of our properties, we changed the name from La Casa to East 3434 so we could appeal to all demographics, not just one. You don't want a name that may limit you in any way. The new name is hip (at least we think so) and appeals to everyone. A logo and name convey an image. Make sure they convey one that is aligned with your business plan.

We also changed the signage and continued that color scheme throughout the property, which gave the building much greater curb appeal. Originally, we had a bland sign that was hard to see because of shrubbery that needed to be trimmed. Now, you can see a more visually stimulating sign from much farther away, and there's much more signage throughout the property. It was hard to find the leasing office before our changes, but now, you can tell the leasing office is the epicenter of the property.

PAINTING

Speaking of curb appeal, painting is a great way to update your property. It doesn't directly go to the bottom line, like water-saving fixtures, but it does play a big role in attracting new residents and retaining current ones, which will push occupancy higher. Even a slight tick higher in economic occupancy will provide a tremendous boost to NOI and value. Sometimes, you can get away with just painting certain sections to highlight them, but if the color scheme is drab and it's been a while, a full paint job is the way to go.

Obviously, painting the interior of a unit is important too. Paying a bit extra for an accent wall can net you a slight bump in rent that totals more than the cost of the extra work.

As we mentioned in Chapter 11 (Renovation Management), curb appeal is important. Well-lit signage, landscaping, exterior paint, and even asphalt repairs make a huge difference. They go a long way in making residents feel proud of the community they live in and a great first impression for potential renters.

INTERIOR UNITS

Interior upgrades are one of the most important parts of any value-add plan. It is important you know the competition and submarket so you don't over-improve your units, causing your return on investment to suffer. If the property is an A or B class apartment community, you are opting for stainless-steel appliances. If it is a C class, you will probably opt for black appliances and save a little money. Are you splurging for a full gut of the unit or just a light value-add? This depends on what condition the unit is in, your business plan, and how much you can push your rents based on the renovations. We'll dive into some of the many upgrades you can do.

Vinyl flooring is a great, inexpensive way to update your units. We like to do vinyl flooring throughout the unit, including bedrooms, living rooms, and upper floors. It saves us money on turns and just looks better. A lot of operators like to keep carpet in the bedrooms or at least on upper floors for noise, but we like to use vinyl flooring throughout.

Pulls on cabinets add a really nice touch and are inexpensive. They will also prolong the life of your cabinets. New lighting fixtures and plumbing fixtures are another low-cost way to improve the look of your units without breaking the bank.

Painting cabinets and refinishing countertops are inexpensive refurbishments, but you need to know your submarket, as we mentioned. Are those acceptable for the rents you are trying to achieve? If not, you may need to splurge on new cabinets and countertops. If your plan is to only paint and resurface countertops, make sure you confirm the cabinets are in good enough shape for just a paint job. There are times you may need to replace the entire cabinet, which can be much more costly and affect your capex budget. You also need to know what your competition is providing and their rents as well. There is a wide range you can spend. Having the ability to buy in bulk helps cut down on those costs.

Backsplashes are a good option to spruce up an apartment. You can purchase a stick-on that looks like tile and is actually pretty nice for only fifty dollars! That would be acceptable for a C property, but as you move up in class, the level of finishes gets more expensive. You need to have real tile for B and up assets.

We like to add washers and dryers in two-bedroom units or greater. Residents are willing to pay a fifty-dollar to seventy-five-dollar rent bump for this. It could take four-plus years for it to pay for itself, but the real gain is the value it brings to the resale. Twelve months of seventy-five dollars divided by a 6 cap is a $15,000 increase in value! Install one hundred units, and that's $1.5 million! This is why we love value-add. There are a ton of options to force appreciation.

UTILITY SAVINGS

Does your property have low-flow toilets, showerheads, and faucets? Changing 128 showerheads cost us only $7,680 but will save us $10,493 per year, according to the green report. If you divide this by a 6 cap, that's a $174,883 value we created by just that one move! We also switched to LED lighting for the exterior at a cost of $6,000, which will save us $2,445 per year. This may not sound like as big of a deal, but it still creates $40,750 in value! We will take that any day of the week. Granted, every property is different, and the numbers are estimations, but you can see how much value this strategy can bring.

A green report will list all the different things you can do to save you or the resident money, the percentage of the savings, and the cost. It will be included in the cost of your loan if you are doing a Fannie Green Program (this program requires you to save 15 percent each on electric and water), or you can hire an outside company to do it for you. Depending on the city/market you are in, you may be able to get rebates for installing some of these items, which reduces your costs even further!

Go to www.bestinclassbook.co to check out what was recommended in the green report and what we did for one of our properties!

AMENITIES

Adding amenities is another way to add value. You may or may not see this go to your bottom line, depending on what you add. The cost of adding amenities can range from a few thousand for a dog park to $100,000 or more to add a nice pool or gym. Adding a few low-cost amenities can go a long way in retaining and attracting new residents. However, space for amenities can be an issue, so you have to be creative sometimes. For example, we're going to get rid of a low-performing vending machine in one of our properties so we have enough room to add a package locker.

Upgrading amenities is also a great option that does not break the bank but goes a long way toward improving your property. One amenity that usually gets upgraded is the pool. Oftentimes, it needs refinishing, or you may opt to update the pool furniture. Sometimes, you can fence in some patios for first floor units, which allows you to charge more for those units. Another option is replacing outdated gym equipment. Each property is different and gives you a bunch of options.

Can you separate yourself from your competitors by adding an amenity, or do you need to add one just to compete? Resident feedback is huge here. What if they want a soccer field and you put in a basketball court that never gets used? Listen to your residents and preferably speak with them when you are in due diligence so you can build their suggestions into your business plan. Thinking about these things is important because residents and potential residents will shop around.

Amenities can also be revenue generating. Package lockers are now more important than ever. Amazon Prime has more than 112 million members in the US at the time of this writing. More deliveries now occur than ever before, and you don't want your property management team burdened with having to deal with packages. Currently in Phoenix, you can charge your residents a one-time fee for a package locker—around twenty-five dollars per person in the household—and five to ten dollars a month depending on the class of your property. Pricing for installing a locker is roughly $120 per unit.

Charging for covered parking or assigned parking is another way to add a little bit to your bottom line. Even if you get 20 percent of the people in a one hundred-unit community to pay twenty dollars a month for parking, that comes to $4,800 a year. That adds $80,000 of value at the time of sale based on a 6 cap. Why wouldn't you want to test that out? Assigned parking does not cost you anything except a little paint, but covered parking does cost about $1,500 per space in our market. However, that would come out of capex and not operating expenses, so you will still see the value added to the NOI and resale.

Now that COVID-19 has rocked our world, you have to

think about how amenities may change and evolve. Perhaps you want to offer mini-gym pods so people can work out by themselves with a few pieces of equipment. Amenities like a grill or picnic area may need to be reserved so cleaning can take place between uses. Or washers and dryers in units may become an even more desired amenity. Think about what may add the most value to your residents' lives when choosing what amenities to add. But one thing is for sure—including amenities in your renovation plan makes sure you are one step ahead of the competition.

As we mentioned in Chapter 11 (Renovation Management), target deferred maintenance so current residents see the changes and are more willing to stay and pay higher rents. It will also save you money in the long run.

GENERAL ADVICE

Adding value to your property is a never-ending process; there are always new ways to innovate, factors to consider, and global changes to account for. For instance, a value-add strategy is not all about what you *do* to a property, it is also about *how* it is managed. A property can be poorly run due to the decisions of the previous owner. Was the previous owner pushing rents? We have seen properties where rents were as much as $300 below market. This happens when an owner falls asleep at the wheel or just cares about maximizing occupancy. Balancing occupancy with pushing rents takes a delicate touch and knowing your business plan. Like we said previously, if we have an occupancy of 95 percent or above, we can hold the line and bring everyone up to market rent. But if we dip below that, we may take a little less to minimize turnover and maximize our cash flow. Typically, our business plan is three to five years, so we can take more of a long approach. If it was shorter, we'd be pushing rents faster at a cost of potentially higher vacancy.

Marketing is another important value-add strategy. Evaluate where every single dollar is spent by reviewing where the leads and conversions are coming from over time and the cost for each one. What marketing can you take advantage of for free? Every city has different results. Put your time, money, and energy into what delivers the most leases by tracking all the steps of leasing.

RUBS is also an excellent way to add value and contribute to your bottom line. This is a method that calculates a resident's utility bill based on a predetermined formula. That formula is typically based on how many bedrooms a unit has but can also be based on square footage and how many occupants or bathrooms are in a unit. Another common strategy is just a flat rate for utilities. The rate can cover water, sewer, trash, electricity, and gas. You won't recover all the money for those expenses, but anything you recover goes straight toward your bottom line. There are companies out there that can handle RUBS for you and recoup up to

95 percent of utility bills. We use this and have been very happy with the results.

RUBS is mainly for master-metered properties, meaning the units are not individually billed. This type of property does not incentivize residents to conserve resources because they know they are not billed by usage, and utility bills can be 15 to 35 percent higher than at an individually metered property.

You'd be surprised how many properties don't use RUBS or include it as part of the rent. Obviously, every submarket is different, so know your market before implementing RUBS. Still, if your market doesn't utilize RUBS, that doesn't mean you can't try. Start small, and see how it plays out. You never know—other apartment complexes may start following suit.

Partnering with a cable/internet provider can be another great way to generate extra revenue. There are a wide variety of options and providers, so do your research before committing. There may also be a way to offer greater efficiencies. We've seen communities that have way too many staff sitting around. If you can reduce a staff person due to economies of scale, that could be a significant savings. Automate as much as you can, and build systems to free up time so your team can be more efficient.

CONCLUSION

There are so many opportunities to add value to your property. You can't tackle all your projects at once, but if you keep saving a little here and adding additional income there, it will add up to a huge jump in the value of your property.

There are many other options that we have not listed here to add value to your property. If you are increasing your NOI every single month, you are on the right path. Keep searching for new and innovative ways to add value. We'll be sure to share what we come up with at www.bestinclassbook.co.

CHAPTER 13

INVESTOR RELATIONS

Good communication is the bridge between confusion and clarity.

—NAT TURNER

Good investor relations are critical if you are looking to scale your real estate business. They may even be more important than performance, believe it or not (it just depends on what your investors look for when they come back to invest).

All that said, you do not need an MBA, expensive tools, or a training program to be good at investor relations. You just need to be consistent, transparent, authentic, and timely! This chapter will explore some of the simple best practices that can increase an investor's trust in you and solidify good investor relations. This is an area that we've seen run the gamut between operators and can play a big role in your long-term success.

RESPONSE TIMES

One of the simplest and most important things to do is respond to your investors promptly. When an investor reaches out, you should respond within twenty-four hours and as soon as you can. We have heard many investors complain about operators who are slow to respond or do not respond at all. This is one of the worst mistakes you can make as an Asset Manager. This infuriates and worries investors; they have placed a tremendous amount of trust in you, and it's only natural they expect a timely response.

Do not ghost your investors, no matter how bad the situation is. If you are away and unable to answer, have a message automatically sent informing them you will get back to them at a certain date. There is no excuse to not be timely in responding to investors, especially in this day and age of instant communication.

REPORTING THROUGH MULTIPLE CHANNELS

With ActiveCampaign or the like, you can communicate with your investors on a consistent basis. "Consistent" means monthly during normal years. For us, that means 10:00 a.m. on the nineteenth of every month. During times of crisis, such as a pandemic, we suggest weekly or bi-weekly communication, at least in the beginning. A well-communicated and transparent email will give your investors confidence in the job you are doing as an Asset Manager.

In our monthly report, we share total income and expenses as well as if we are above or below budget. If we are off by a lot, we go into more detail about what is going on and how we are fixing it. Like we said, be transparent. Communicate your occupancy and preleased occupancy as well. Let your investors know where you stand on your business plan. We provide links to a Google Drive for things such as our project list timeline, pertinent articles about the local area, pictures of renovations, and data on the property to fill out a statement of real estate owned. We also include links to the quarterly financials and rent rolls. It is not just about data and information regarding your property; it is about adding value to your investors.

In this email, you need to communicate both good and bad news. Sorry, you cannot just send the good news, but if you communicate how you are taking action to fix a situation and why it happened, it will instill confidence in your investors. Do not make excuses, and do not run away from a bad situation. Things do not always go as planned, and an experienced investor will understand that as long as you communicate the bad news right away and have a detailed plan of action about how to get back on track. Do not sit on it or sweep it under the rug because eventually, it will come out, and you will wish you were upfront with your investors. Being transparent is paramount.

This is a relationship business. You have to pull back the curtain and let the investor in. A well-crafted email will save you time because you have answered every possible question an investor might ask. We like to overcommunicate. An investor can always choose not to read the information; quite often, they may not read everything you send them. That is okay. It is about providing enough information to please *all* your investors, especially the ones who like to ask many questions. Imagine you have invested your money in a syndication and ask yourself, "What type of information would I like to receive?"

Here is an example of one of our emails to investors:

Investors,

Below is an update on November collections:

As of Friday, November 13, we have collected ~95% of the scheduled rents.

In comparison to October, we are trending about 6% ahead of last month's collections.

Currently, there are two residents that have not paid their November rent. Of these two, we hope to collect from one, which would result in collecting ~97% of the rents this month, which is ahead of last month.

At this point, there have been zero cases of COVID-19 reported at the property.

Financials

Below is the monthly update for the month of October:

Total Income: $24,028 ($1,528 above budget)
Expenses: $11,041 ($348 under budget)
Net Operating Income: $12,987 ($1,876 above budget)
YTD Net Operating Income: $67,450 ($14,971 above budget)
Total Net Operating Income to Budget: $43,397 above
Current Occupancy: 92.86 percent (up from 88.10 percent)
Preleased Occupancy: 95.24 percent (down from 100 percent)

Updates

Great news! We received approval for the grant we applied for about two months ago in the amount of $10,627! This grant was for assistance to landlords for non-paying renters. This should be hitting our bank account soon and will be recorded in either the November or December P&L depending on when the funds are received.

More great news! We have also received approval for a water rebate from the City of Tucson for installing low-flow toilets on the property. The amount has yet to be determined, but we should be receiving this before the end of the year as well.

Click here for data on the property in order to complete your Statement of Real Estate Owned.

Click here to see the updated Project List Timeline.

We have also instituted quarterly Zoom meetings to discuss the property. The meeting can last as little as twenty minutes, but we are giving our investors an opportunity to ask any questions they may have and allow us another avenue to communicate how things are progressing. Different investors prefer different ways to digest information, so you want to provide multiple avenues to connect with all your investors.

CARING MATTERS

Monthly emails are not the only way you want to communicate with your investors. Individual quarterly calls to investors, which are different from the group quarterly Zoom meetings, continue to strengthen your relationship and keep you top of mind when they or a friend of theirs are looking to invest. It is important that when you do talk to an investor, you discuss more than just business. Ask how they are doing, about their kids, about their hobbies—build a real relationship. This is about actually caring, and not just because they invested in your deal (they will see through that). It is easy to put off these quarterly calls, but those who are consistent will reap the rewards.

Besides the monthly newsletters, quarterly Zoom meetings, and quarterly calls, consider reaching out on their birthday, a child's graduation, an anniversary, or a timely event. It is critical you are authentic. Do not reach out just because you want them to invest. Reach out because you care. During the holidays, it is always a good idea to send a card at the very least. If you want to go further, send a thoughtful gift. These small gestures will go a long way in building a strong relationship. You do not just want to reach out when you have a deal; going the extra mile will separate you from others and make your investors feel special.

Another thing we like to do is host a lunch or dinner with our investors when we close a property. This does not need to cost you a lot, and a little bit spent will pay huge dividends in the long run. We know others that host big, fancy dinners and a weekend of activities. Do what is most comfortable for you.

We have been praised countless times by our investors for the way we communicate with them and how much we care.

These are huge differentiators. How are you differentiating from other owners?

FIDUCIARY RESPONSIBILITY

Investor relations are not solely about communication. You are a fiduciary to your investors' money, so you need to make decisions that take into account the interests of your investors first. It is a huge responsibility to manage an asset that people have invested their hard-earned money in, no matter how small the property or investment. Every decision you make should be made with their interests in mind.

For example, a new sponsor might be eager to have a deal go full cycle and push for a sale when perhaps he has not performed to the level he promised in the offering. Certainly, if you can deliver great returns in a short period of time, it's hard to turn down an offer, but engage with your investors, find out what they want (particularly if you are new to this business). You must be aligned with their goals, and that starts with the business plan.

INVESTOR PORTAL

We recommend an investor portal if you are serious about being an Asset Manager. It is useful to put K-1s there, and you can send out investor communications from it. You can also utilize it for any upcoming deal you may have to manage and track the capital you raise. Investors can update their banking information for distributions, track investment performance, and have all their signed documents in one place. Trust us; if you do not have a portal, investors will keep asking for this information, so a portal will save you a lot of time in the long run.

DISTRIBUTIONS

Distributions vary depending on your business plan. If it is a value-add play, you may not have distributions for at least six months. You can opt for monthly or quarterly distributions, but this decision is usually made when you are putting together your operating agreement.

Before making your first distribution, verify all the banking information is correct for all your investors. Some people change their bank often, so it is better to fix any potential problems on the front end. Other people may opt to switch to an automated clearing house (ACH) or vice versa. A good investor portal makes this quite easy to manage.

Most investors are anxious for that first distribution. To them, if they get that check, they feel things are going well. That is not to say send a distribution check even when you should not. Remember, transparency is a must if you want to be in this business for the long haul. You need to manage your cash reserves; you never want to make a distribution and then soon after, have a capital call. A generally accepted rule is to have three to six months of operating capital in reserve. This helps to insure against the unknown, like a natural disaster or pandemic.

CONCLUSION

Without good investor relations, you will be managing fewer assets as time goes on. You do not need 1,000 investors if you treat your current investors the right way and with the respect they deserve. You may be better served by having one hundred raving fans than 1,000 who just know your name. One hundred investors who put an average of $75,000 in every deal comes to $7.5 million. That will allow you to close a lot of deals. Remember, be consistent, transparent, timely, and authentic, and well-thought-out communication is key to keeping your investors happy.

CHAPTER 14

CURVEBALLS

Focus on the solution, not the problem.

—JIM ROHN

There are always curveballs in life. No matter how careful you are and how much risk mitigation you do, there will always be events you cannot predict, such as COVID-19. People expected a downturn was coming—the economy had been growing for an unprecedented length of time— but no one could have predicted the black swan event or its potential length.

When faced with curveballs, there are those who will leap to action. They will be creative and pivot to make the best of the situation. There are others, however, who are set in their ways and slow to act; they will most likely fail in their endeavors. If you are reading this book, it is likely you belong to the first group and like to take action to see results.

As a basic rule, remember to be conservative in your underwriting, which gives you the cushion you need to withstand curveballs. You need to have that safety net. If you do not use long-term historical norms, you might be hurting in a time of crisis. In this chapter, we'll explore principles to help you prepare for and handle curveballs.

FACE CURVEBALLS HEAD-ON

One of the most important things to do when you encounter a curveball is to face the issue head-on. This is not a time to bury your head in the sand and hope it goes away or work in a silo. Remember, it will pass, and do not freak out. Take a deep breath, and lay out a plan with your team; it will help you get through it. This is a time to overcommunicate with your investors. As we discuss in Chapter 13 (Investor Relations), tell your investors the issue and how you are fixing it. Double down on your communication at this point. Your investors need to be kept in the loop. A lack of communication will only waste extra time and create frustration, as investors will reach out wondering what is going on.

The quote at the beginning of the chapter, "Focus on the solution, not the problem," is an important mindset to have in a time of crisis. Handle what you can control, and keep your team focused on that.

Go back to the stress test you did in your underwriting. (You did do a stress test, right? If not, now is a good time to do one.) What is the minimum amount of income you need to cover all your expenses and debt service? What is the minimum economic occupancy you need to survive, and how many months of reserves do you have to cover the issue? Do you have to dig into your renovations budget to cover the losses you may incur? That is not ideal, but if it means keeping your property afloat, it is a good option.

From an asset management standpoint, we have to focus on everyone's health and well-being first and foremost when we are in a crisis situation. After that, we are no longer looking to produce wealth for investors; we are looking at preserving capital.

- Can we reduce any expenses?
- Is this just a two-month blip and then we are on again?
- Do we need to reevaluate the value-add plan we have put in place?
- Do we need to completely reevaluate what that value-add plan means?
- What did our original PPM state, and is there any ability to raise additional equity in there if it came to that?
- What is our normal delinquency rate?

- Are rent collections every five days trending up or down month over month?
- How far off are we on the rent collection trends?

We will also evaluate our KPIs daily to identify issues. For example, if we are seeing a big drop off in inquiries for available units, obviously, that's a red flag. Evaluate all your data frequently, as you will have to make adjustments on the fly during a crisis.

In a crisis, we focus on occupancy, bringing in more leads, potentially offering concessions, renewing current residents, and being strategic about how we offer those concessions. During COVID-19, we could not use eviction as a threat because there was a moratorium. Bringing in leads was difficult, as we were not getting walk-ins, so we had to increase our online marketing, offer 3-D virtual tours, and ensure everything was updated across all our platforms. Just because people are on lockdown does not mean the team sits idly by. We worked with residents to avoid turnover. The team was consistently taking action. If something was not working, they would try something else (which is a recurring theme of the book).

You also have to be careful about how you lease up your apartments because it can be difficult to evict residents if they are not paying. If you are just going to offer the biggest concession in the world, who are you attracting and what leverage do you have to pull if you're not able to evict them? Concessions need to be handled in an empathetic but strategic manner. You want to help people get into your apartments but do not want residents to take advantage.

During the beginning of the COVID-19 crisis, we only handled the most urgent work orders, and they were done with the strictest of care. The leasing office was closed, but leasing staff worked out of it. We started with virtual tours. After a while, we were able to leave units open for potential residents to tour by themselves. We limited community interactions as much as possible and focused on resolving our delinquency.

You need to put all non-urgent items on hold and triage things. Safety is the most important priority. Then, you have to decide what else needs to happen to continue operations at the bare minimum. Our weekly calls with property management turned into daily check-ins. Working together as a team is more critical during a crisis than at other times.

PROPERTY MANAGEMENT

You also need to make sure your property management company has a disaster plan. Has everyone been trained on the plan and understands it? You never know when a crisis may happen, but you want your team to be able to leap into action and deal with a situation as best they can.

Depending on the location of your property, your team may or may not be more equipped to handle a particular crisis. For instance, Florida has had 120 hurricanes in the last 160 years, so you would think they would be prepared for that. California, on the other hand, does not have hurricanes. They have their own natural disasters to worry about, like fires and earthquakes. You also want to make sure you are covered insurance wise for natural disasters that could happen in the areas in which you invest. When you are using other people's money, our theory is to opt for the additional coverage because you don't want to face the burden of being underinsured.

When surprises happen, it is likely your property management company will have some experience in managing the situation (assuming they have been around a while). Do not be afraid to lean on them and their legal team—that is what you are paying your property management company for. They are literally your boots on the ground. They will be the ones talking to your residents and working through the situation. Everyone will be under stress when curveballs occur, so be sympathetic about it. Be a cheerleader and a problem solver, and you will be amazed what can be accomplished.

WORKING WITH RESIDENTS

During difficult times, work with residents; make sure your

property management company has a system for this. For example, arrange for a middle-assistance program for kids, like a nonprofit that comes to your property six days a week and gives meals to kids. You gain a lot of goodwill from residents and are helping them during these difficult times.

The other thing you can do is not only let residents know where they can go for rent-assistance programs but go the extra mile and make an effort to really help them get the assistance they need. Maybe you can set up a computer station and say, "Why don't you come to the office? We'll file it for you, we'll provide you the guidance, and we will help you." Remember, you may have residents that are not particularly good with technology, and helping them acquire monetary assistance is good for you both. We sent weekly emails to each resident letting them know about new assistance programs and how to get access to them during COVID-19. They really appreciated the proactiveness and extra communication during this time. We made them feel safe and valued.

When COVID-19 hit, we were communicating with our property management team daily. We were all sharing resources and trying to stay on top of the everchanging rules and situation. However, you do not want to rely solely on your property management team—you definitely want to seek other input as well. Most likely, others have been through a similar situation before or the entire region is facing the same crisis, so it is great to hear what others are doing. There is no shame in copying best practices.

BEING WELL CAPITALIZED

Being well capitalized is essential to getting through tough times. "Well capitalized" means not using cash flow to pay for capex; you need to raise all that money upfront. If you rely on cash flow and it dries up, you have no way to execute the rest of your business plan. Being well capitalized also means having reserves, which again, you raise upfront. The older the property, the more reserves you hold per unit to fix things; this allows you to be flexible during a crisis/curveball and either continue with your plan or pivot based on what you are seeing in the market. Those who are not well capitalized when a curveball arrives will only have one option: hope and pray they make it out okay. You, on the other hand, may be able to take advantage of this situation and position your property ahead of the competition.

INSURANCE

Insurance may be something you need during a time of crisis. Maybe you had a fire on the property or some type of major damage. No one likes reading their insurance policy—you just get the policy they suggest and be done with it, right? We are also guilty as charged. But you should be smarter. You need to work with someone you trust and who is looking out for your particular needs, not someone who just wants to quickly write you a policy. Typically, there's a lot of extra coverages you can get for a very small price, so make sure you at least inquire about the different options so you can weigh what is worth adding and what is not. You may also want to opt for a higher deductible to save some money on that end. It's not worth putting in for small claims, as your insurance costs will probably go up, so having a higher deductible is a great option.

The terms "excess insurance" and "umbrella insurance" are often used interchangeably, and although they operate in the same way, they are not the same. An excess liability policy provides an increased limit over just one specific line of coverage. In the case of an operator, that is likely your premises liability. An umbrella policy, while costlier, offers more flexibility to extend limits over multiple liability policies, like professional, commercial auto, errors and omissions, etc. Most agency loans will require this additional coverage.

Here is an example of how it could work if you had a commercial liability policy with a $1 million per occurrence limit and a commercial umbrella policy with a $3 million limit. A fire occurs at one of your properties, resulting in the death of a resident. You get sued for negligence by a family member, and the judge awards them a $2.5 million judgment. The first $1 million gets paid out by your underlying commercial liability policy minus legal fees then $1.5 million plus the legal fees comes out of your umbrella policy, and your included coverage extends to legal defense fees. If you did not have the umbrella policy, your business assets would be responsible for the additional $1.5 million, but your personal assets would still be protected.

CONCLUSION

Dealing with curveballs starts in the underwriting phase. You prepare yourself to survive and thrive with conservative underwriting and capital reserves or walk a dangerous tight rope where you *may* be okay if everything runs perfectly—but that is a recipe for failure. Do yourself and your investors a favor and plan for the worst so you can perform your best even in the worst times. Face curveballs head-on, and leverage your property management team. It is much easier to tackle an obstacle knowing others are with you every step of the way. No one can predict everything that may happen, but there is always a solution. If you can minimize the damage of curveballs, you will succeed in everything you do in life and have the makings of an excellent Asset Manager.

CHAPTER 15

TAXES

The Seven Ps—Proper Prior Planning Prevents Pitiful Poor Performance.

—DON MEYER

Taxes are often overlooked when you are initially underwriting a multifamily opportunity as well as during the management of the property. However, it is an important detail that should not be taken lightly. Not only do taxes affect you and your sponsorship team, but they also affect each and every one of your investors. You need to have a good understanding of how taxes work within a syndication or apartment investment.

More importantly, you must have a great CPA who specializes and has extensive experience in working in real estate, specifically the type of real estate model you invest with.

The first time we hired a real estate-focused CPA firm, they immediately saved us $3,000 just by reviewing the returns from previous years. You have to have the mindset of focusing on what the CPA will save you on your taxes over the long term rather than what that person is costing you now. Good CPAs can be expensive but are usually well worth the cost. In addition, there are just too many changes to the tax code every year for you to keep track of yourself. Having an expert CPA on your team who reviews these changes and has a deep understanding of them is a must.

NOTE: We are not tax professionals or CPAs; you need to consult with a tax professional. This chapter is for informational purposes only and not to be used as actual tax advice.

WHERE TO BEGIN

In this chapter, we'll cover some of the tax basics you should know. As we've mentioned throughout this book, hiring professionals is important, but it's equally important for you to have a grasp on the basics so you know how to manage your property, ask the right questions, and identify where things are slipping.

The first thing for syndicators to understand when it comes to taxes is what you are trying to accomplish with your deals. Are you trying to tax optimize this deal, are you fine not tax optimizing, or do you simply want to break even? If you are asking yourself, "Why would someone just want to break even?" it's because everyone's tax situation is different. You will need to know what is best for you and your investors. Just this can help answer a lot of questions for you, such as whether or not you perform a cost segregation on your properties or how you are going to step through the expenditures for capex and other related items. Are you going to analyze them in detail to determine if they are repairs or if they are capex?

A cost segregation is the strategic process where a cost segregation consultant analyzes commercial real estate to determine whether identifying and segregating certain components of the property as personal property (Section 1245 Property) that are separate and distinct from the real property (Section 1250 Property) will produce any accelerated depreciation benefits for income tax purposes. Real estate investors can receive immediate expensing of certain five-, seven-, and fifteen-year properties. As a result, you and your investors can substantially increase cash flow by segregating these property costs and enjoy tremendous tax benefits from accelerated depreciation deductions and easier write-offs when an asset becomes obsolete, broken, or destroyed. Granted, tax laws and this strategy may change at some point.

We will not get into the details of cost segregation in this chapter, but it is something you should definitely be aware of. Depending on your business plan and hold period, it is a tool you should be utilizing. Please consult your CPA or a cost segregation expert for more information.

THREE BIG TAX CONSIDERATIONS

When it comes to taxes, there are three big tax considerations an Asset Manager should keep in mind at the time we wrote this book. The very first thing is understanding the tax attributes of the deal you're trying to push to your investors as well as what type of investors you have in your deal. Are they mainly real estate professionals that can claim the losses if they run an aggregation at their own personal levels? Are they a bunch of Silicon Valley investors who have full-time jobs that can never claim the losses? Or are they a mix of both? This will help you understand what your tax strategy should ultimately be. Again, as we mentioned, are you trying to maximize losses or do you just want to break even from a tax perspective? Of course, your CPA will help you through this, but you will need to provide them with the relevant information to make an informed decision.

The second most important thing as it pertains to taxes is understanding the 2013 tangible property regulations. You don't have to know them inside and out, but the 2013 tangible property regulations are going to tell you how you can deduct expenditures. Can you capitalize, should you be capitalizing them, or can you deduct the expenditures as a repair?

For example, say you have a ten-unit apartment complex, all units are under one roof, and all units have their own HVAC unit. If you replace one HVAC unit, some CPAs, Asset Managers, and property managers will capitalize the HVAC unit to the balance sheet. When you look at the 2013 tangible property regulations, you realize if you look at the entire HVAC system, that one HVAC unit was not a material improvement to the HVAC system as a whole, so you can actually *deduct* it! It goes back again to what you are trying to do (maximize taxes, break even, etc.). You get some flexibility there, but just understanding where you *can* get that flexibility is really key.

The last thing is the de minimis safe harbor election, which is incredible! This is also within the 2013 tangible property rights, but many people do not even know it exists. The de minimis safe harbor election is simply an administrative convenience that generally allows you to elect to deduct small dollar expenditures for the acquisition or production of property that otherwise must be capitalized under the general rules. This keeps you from capitalizing, for example, a $500 appliance and small things like that. You just write it all off, you elect the de minimis safe harbor, and you call it a day. Again, consult a CPA, as this is not something you should be doing yourself, but it's important you know it exists, which is the main objective of this chapter.

Once again, here are the three big tax considerations Asset Managers should pay attention to:

1. Understand your investors and what you are trying to accomplish.
2. 2013 tangible property regulations
3. De minimis safe harbor election

Overwhelmed or confused yet? So are we! That is why you need to have an expert CPA on your team. Be sure to schedule a consult with a CPA before you even have a property to set yourself up the right way. Be organized from the start; it will make your life much easier.

TAXES DURING THE DUE DILIGENCE PHASE

Once you are closing in on a property, your CPA should be brought in during due diligence (so before you even own the property). They will want to look at the operating agreement. The operating agreement has a lot of tax attributes in it, and you'll need to answer several questions:

- How do you split distributions?
- How do you split gain?
- How do you split income and losses?

- How is all that allocated?
- What does that mean for the limited partners and the general partners?
- How should your overall tax strategy come into play?

It really all starts with that operating agreement, and you should have your CPA brought in to assist with the buildout.

During the due diligence phase, before the syndicate even closes on the deal, you should typically already have a rough idea of the tax strategy you want to employ. It's not necessarily a document you're going to hand to the investors, but it is sitting down with your CPA and going over questions such as:

- Are you going to perform a cost segregation?
- Do you want to maximize the losses coming out of this deal?
- If so, what do you need to look for whenever you're doing any capex or repairs?
- Do you need to elect out of business interest limitations?

BUSINESS INTEREST LIMITATIONS

Speaking of, the business interest limitations were actually modified in 2020 with the CARES Act. They are limitations on interest you are allowed to deduct if you are a qualifying business within that section of the code. That is a big deal for syndications because syndications have a lot of interest from their mortgages. This would be considered business interest. As we mentioned before, these are things that are extremely important to you and your investors. If you do not have an expert CPA on your team, these are the types of things that will slip through the cracks.

When business interest limitations came out, the real estate industry didn't really pay much attention to them. But when you do more research and understand how it works and interplays with other sections of the code, you actually realize almost every single syndication has to worry about business interest limitations. Here's why: there's a provision of the code that says if you're a tax shelter, you are subject to the business interest limitations.

A tax shelter is any partnership that allocates its losses to limited partners that make up more than 35 percent of the deal. So, for example, if you are a general partner and you have less than 65 percent of the deal allocated to the general partnership, the limited partners have 35 percent or more of the deal. If you, as the general partner, have losses from a cost segregation or losses in general that you allocate to the limited partners who own, again, more than 35 percent of the deal, you are subject to business interest limitations (these are most syndications).

According to our CPA, there were a lot of mistakes made

in 2018 by CPAs who didn't even know this was something they had to worry about. Remember, everything about your taxes is fine until it's not (meaning you're audited). Be proactive, and save yourself and your investors time, money, and stress. The nice thing for syndications and funds is you can elect out of the business interest limitations as an electing real property trade or business.

Now, there are challenges with electing out of business interest limitations. You will want to discuss this with your CPA so you know about them in advance. The timing of the election is definitely important, and it varies deal to deal. It might be year one, it might be year two, or it might be a future year. You just have to figure out when it is going to be for your specific syndication.

WHAT IS A K-1?

This is another area you will want to make sure you have at least a general understanding of, as we assure you there will be questions from your investors about their K-1. A K-1 is the partner's summary of the partnership's activity. For example, if three people are partners, your CPA will prepare a Form 1065, which is the partnership tax return. Then, each one of the partners will receive a K-1, which is a supplemental form to the Form 1065. You'll receive a K-1 that summarizes the partnership's activity and allocates it to you for your ownership stakes. You can see a sample K-1 at www.bestinclassbook.co.

The most important part of any K-1 you receive is your ownership stake (that's on the left-hand side of the K-1). You need to make sure that's correct. You're also going to check any liabilities allocated to you, either recourse or non-recourse. You need to make sure that is also correct. Then, you need to review the capital account analysis, which is going to show you what you put into the deal and what you're taking out of the deal in terms of distributions as well as how the net profit or losses have affected your capital account.

This all is critical because sometimes syndications switch CPAs, and you need to confirm your new CPA carries this information over as effectively as they should. This is important because if the partnership liquidates at some later point and pays out gains, they are going to have to first drop your capital account to zero.

If you put $50,000 into a partnership, your capital account is $50,000. If the partnership liquidates and has a gain, it has to first pay you back your $50,000 before it's allowed to distribute gain to anybody else. You need to track your capital account balance on a year-to-year basis. That is the number one thing for limited partners to understand—to make sure the K-1 is correct—and it's your job to help them understand this.

The right-hand side of the K-1 is income and loss information. Typically, if you are investing in a syndication, you're going to look at Box 2—that's net rental real estate income or loss. Then in Box 20, you are going to see other information, such as qualified business income (QBI). You will want to discuss this information with your CPA.

For example, let's say the syndicate states you lost a $100,000, and that $100,000 is a negative QBI adjustment. If you're not a real estate professional (most investors are not), you can't take the loss. It becomes suspended, as it is a passive loss. Now, you are looking at passive activity loss limitations. Because it is a negative QBI adjustment, it actually reduces your business income.

You cannot take the loss, but you also get a lower 20 percent passive reduction. Box 20 on the K-1 will show you that information. It is a summary statement that shows you your allocable share of the partnership activities. There are many more pieces to the K-1 that we will not cover here, but the biggest thing you need to clearly track is that capital account on an ongoing basis.

REAL ESTATE PROFESSIONAL DESIGNATION

As an Asset Manager or apartment owner, you may qualify for real estate professional designation. The current definition of a real estate professional is a person that must provide more than one-half of his or her total personal services in real property trades or businesses in which he or she materially participates and performs more than 750 hours of services during the tax year. If you qualify for this designation, it has huge benefits, one of which is being able to deduct 100 percent of your rental depreciation and "losses" against *any* other type of income on the front page of your 1040. If you are a real estate professional, you will need to track your hours to prove you qualify. Yes, even if this is your full-time job. If you are audited, the IRS is going to ask for proof of where your time is being spent. We use a tool called Toggl, but there are many other tools out there. The main thing is to track your hours to prove you are, in fact, a real estate professional.

CONCLUSION

As you can see, taxes are no joke and should be taken very seriously. Although you'll be hiring a CPA to do this work for you, you will still need an understanding of how taxes play a part in your business. If you don't have the slightest clue, how are you supposed to ask your CPA the right questions and be sure your CPA is the right person for your team?

One last thing to mention as we close out this chapter. In the opening, we talked about how taxes often get lost in the underwriting of an opportunity. Below are three examples of these often-missed items:

1. Don't forget to budget for your yearly taxes. For first year setup, this can run several thousands of dollars or more depending on the structure and number of investors.
2. Lenders charge yearly fees as well. Be sure to ask your lender what its yearly charges will be.
3. Keep track of *all* expenses!

CHAPTER 16

DISPOSITION

Always start at the end before you begin...A professional investor always has an exit strategy before they invest... Knowing your exit strategy is an important investment fundamental.

—ROBERT KIYOSAKI

Hopefully, it will be your choice as an Asset Manager to sell because you are getting a price for your property above and beyond what you projected. We say "hopefully" because you do not want to be the Asset Manager burned by having to sell when you are not ready. Perhaps a loan was too short term or you were undercapitalized. Being able to decide when to sell on your own terms—with the investors' best interests in mind, of course—is obviously your goal.

There are many different types of business plans out there. Some investors want to keep refinancing and get to a point of infinite returns. Others want to sell quickly if they can get the NOI to spike or market conditions become favorable. Many like to enjoy cash flow and opt for a five- to seven-year plan. Are you positioning to sell it as a value-add if you are not fully stabilized and have a lot of loss to lease to still burn off? Whatever your exit strategy is, it is best to be a little flexible to deal with curveballs or take advantage of market conditions.

Remember, the future is unpredictable. We have seen people sell their five-year plan properties after only eighteen months because they hit their target returns. We have also seen Asset Managers struggle through their plan for many years before being able to salvage the investment at disposition due to favorable market conditions. You cannot control what the future holds, but you can control learning and practicing the best asset management methods. This is what we've aimed to provide in this book.

Throughout this book, we've taken you on a journey from before you purchase your property to maximizing value while owning it. Now, we'll delve into what it looks like at the end of the hold period.

PREPAYMENT PENALTIES

One of the things a lot of new Asset Managers forget to think about or just put off in order to get the deal is the prepayment penalty. We have seen many operators who want to sell their property but are unable to due to the pre-payment penalty. There are a bunch of factors you have to consider when you pick your loan. Are you looking for the best rate, the most proceeds, the greatest flexibility, or some combination of the three that aligns with your business plan? Some operators opt for a thirty-to-forty basis points decrease in interest rate by opting for a less flexible loan and do not worry about the penalty it will cost them to sell before the loan is due. They grab the lower interest rate to boost their internal rate of returns—and the income earned on the amount invested (cash on cash)—so they can sell the deal to investors. But they fail to take into account they may be unable to sell the property when they want to. If you are a long-term holder, the prepayment penalty is less of an issue.

There are different kinds of prepayment penalties depending on your loan type. We will try and venture down the path of explaining prepayment penalties without going down a rabbit hole.

YIELD MAINTENANCE

A yield maintenance prepayment penalty is common in larger loans. Essentially, it guarantees the lender will get the same yield on the loan even if the loan is paid off before the scheduled maturity date. If the loan is paid off early, the yield maintenance prepayment penalty is then calculated based on a percentage of the amount of principal being prepaid or by multiplying the present value of remaining loan payments by the difference between the loan interest rate and the Treasury rate of the same duration.

When interest rates are falling or stable, a yield maintenance prepayment penalty can be a more expensive alternative for a borrower as opposed to a step-down penalty (which is best for those who seek a shorter-term loan). For example, a yield maintenance prepayment penalty can be as steep as 25 percent (or even more) of the original loan amount; this is huge! Opting for yield maintenance may benefit you on the front end, but there are many operators who no longer have the option to sell because of the severity of these prepayment penalties. When it comes to your real estate journey, begin with the end in mind, and choose carefully.

STEP DOWN

A step-down prepayment penalty sounds just like it is. On a ten-year loan, you may have a 5 percent prepayment penalty in years one and two, 4 percent in years three and four, 3 percent in years five and six, and so on. They do vary, so make sure the step-down aligns with your business plan. Knowing the cost of the prepayment penalty upfront allows you to at least plan and know exactly what your prepayment amount will be based on the year of sale. This is as compared to a yield maintenance penalty, where you have no control over the cost of the penalty since it's tied to current rates. This prepayment penalty is at least predictable.

FLOATING RATE

Another option is a floating-rate loan or adjustable-rate. They usually have a one-year lockout period but only a 1 percent prepayment penalty after that, which is great if you think you may exit earlier and are confident rates won't rise much. The rates usually have a floor, meaning they won't fall below a certain percentage, but they could rise. You can buy an interest rate cap, or ceiling, to minimize your downside from rates rising. The cost all depends on the size of the loan, length of the cap, and interest rate you are capping the rate at. Again, terms vary between programs and market conditions. One other thing to note: floating-rate loans are typically not offered for agency small-balance loans, which are under $5 to $6 million.

A website we use to calculate the cost of a cap on a floating-rate loan is: www.chathamfinancial.com/technology/interest-rate-cap-calculator.

DEFEASANCE

Defeasance is another option for a loan, but we do not

recommend it. It is confusing to understand and has large prepayment penalties. Defeasance refers to the replacement of the collateral of a loan with securities that will offer a lender an equivalent return. Defeasance usually will require an expert consultant to guide you.

As you can see, there are many options out there and a lot to consider when getting a loan, as the prepayment penalties can really affect the returns to your investors. Remember the quote at the beginning of this chapter: "Always start at the end before you begin. A professional investor always has an exit strategy before they invest. Knowing your exit strategy is an important investment fundamental."

ASSESSING THE VALUE OF YOUR PROPERTY

When you want to assess the value of your property, you reach out to a broker to get a broker opinion of value (BOV). The BOV will vary a bit between brokers—some may be overly aggressive to get your business—but based on the estimated number you get, you can calculate the return to investors after closing costs and loan repayment. If it is close to target, you can send a formal communication to your investors asking whether they are in favor of selling or not. Getting a BOV is a continual thing where you are constantly monitoring what's going on in the marketplace.

Just because you get a great BOV does not mean you should

hurry up and sell. Perhaps you want to delay the sale of your property if your loan is not maturing soon, there's a new local employer that announced they are expanding in the area, or you think rent rates will outpace the current growth rate. Maybe you are not yet at a stabilized T12, and waiting a few more months will increase your value. There are many factors to weigh before selling.

Typically, you would use the same broker you bought the deal from. This is just good business practice, and hopefully, you've built up a good rapport and trust over time with this broker so you can have a very realistic discussion about your BOV. However, there are times when it just does not make sense to use the same broker you bought the property from. Maybe the original broker does not typically handle multi-family properties or works for a company that would not fit the type of asset you have now brought it up to. Maybe the broker has a small network or his/her business has fallen off for some reason. It is a difficult decision, but at the end of the day, you ultimately have to pick the best broker for the property.

Whatever broker you choose, you need to strategize about positioning the property. Do you need to upgrade a few units to a higher renovation level to create a value-add play for your property? Is it best to wait a few more months to burn off more loss to lease and sell it as a turnkey asset? You'll also need to discuss any potential red flags a buyer may encounter, and you need to be prepared for the possibility a buyer may want to re-trade (ask for a discount) due to those red flags. Your specific market conditions will dictate how you approach some of these topics.

When you are close to that total return based on the BOV, it means your property may be ready to sell. We know some operators target 70 percent return to investors after all expenses of a sale are factored in. Operators typically have a clause in the operating agreement that allows them to sell if they have somewhere between 50 and 80 percent of the vote from their investors. Remember, the percentage of vote is dependent on ownership percentage and not by an equal vote per person.

PREPARING TO SELL

If you have enough percentage in favor of selling the property, you are ready to go from there. You still need help from your staff, so make sure you have a bonus plan for them. We have seen different ways to do this, but one of the most common is to give the staff one month's salary as a bonus. Some owners prefer not to tell their staff too early, as it could have a negative effect on performance; they may start looking for new jobs. We feel open and honest communication is always the best way to go; incentivize and work together. Having a good relationship with the management company, if it is a third party, goes a long way as well. We all are in this business for the long haul, right? You never want to burn a bridge with a management company or your staff because you will be buying another property down the road. You need those people.

This would be a good time to reach out to your lender and get the actual amount of your prepayment penalty in writing. Usually, this will be good for thirty days. We were in a Best and Final to purchase a property and had spent countless hours working on this deal when, at the eleventh hour, the seller realized their penalty was more than three times higher than they originally thought. The deal was dead, as the seller did not want to absorb that additional cost nor did any buyer. Be prepared. This frustrated all the parties involved because they should have had everything in order.

One of the biggest questions we hear is "How do you select the right buyer?" Surety to close is very important. You do not want to waste three months or longer and not have that person close. You will want to check the buyer's track record, where the money is coming from, and whether they are putting up hard money (which varies from market to market and with the economic cycle). Hopefully, your broker will help you, but at the end of the day, it will be your choice. We have seen buyers just go for the highest sale price and not worry about surety to close (although, just because someone offers the highest price does not mean they will *not* close). Another factor to consider is working with a 1031 buyer, as timing could be an issue. Additionally, you should look for where the potential buyer's capital is sourced, how much they can typically take on per year, and if they have any current or recent projects that may result in some of their capital being dried up for the time being. As you can see, there are a lot of things to consider.

Visit www.bestinclassbook.co to see a sample Buyer Questionnaire from a broker so you can gain their perspective on the things they like to see from a potential buyer.

We have seen people sell their properties because they worked their way up to having 99 percent of the units leased and there was minimal turnover coming the following month, so income would spike. This takes a lot of work and strategizing—really maximizing your NOI on your T1 and T3—but if you can achieve it, you can drive up the price of your property. Additionally, if you can maintain that high NOI, the buyer could use it to maximize loan proceeds. So, if you can time things right in a seller's market, you can really take advantage of it.

It's key to be in tune to what is going on operationally on all your assets and how that coincides with the current market conditions. Additionally, you need to know what the returns will be for your investors after all the expenses have been paid. That combination can determine a good time to go to market and sell. Obviously, you need to have a plan. Things change, though, and you have to roll with the punches as well.

You may torture yourself wondering if this is the best time to sell or not. Should you wait? Will the market get better? You are just going to have to make a decision based on the available information you have in front of you right now. The future is uncertain. The further out you go, the less certain it is going to be. We know a lot of syndicators who sold deals in 2015, 2016, and 2017 that would have made a lot more money if they had just held a little bit longer. Still, it *was* a great return at the time. You also do not want to sell just to go full cycle if it's not in the best interests of your investors. Yes, it is important when you are new in the business to get that track record of going full cycle. But if your investors are not happy about it, they will not come back.

Remember the deal is never done until the wire goes through and the sale records. A friend of ours learned this the hard way. Even though their deal was all but done and they thought for sure it was going to close, it fell apart two days before it was supposed to close. You have to make sure you're focusing on operations throughout the entire time in escrow because (1) the deal may not close, and (2) if you mess up your operations, it could impact your buyer's loan proceeds and terms. This is why it is critical you maintain your collections and NOI. Run it like you are going to own it regardless of whether it's in escrow or not.

Make sure you look at the payables you still have outstanding. Do not overdistribute the money to your investors. Also, make sure you talk to the management company to have a good sense of what's going to be payables. Ensure you set aside enough money to pay your CPA, file the final tax return, pay any sort of state franchise tax you might owe, and cover anything else needed to wind the entity down. Remember, you never want to try to get money back from investors. Pad that holdback number a little bit so you have enough margin for error in case something comes out of left field; this way, you won't have to claw back cash from your investors.

EXIT STRATEGIES

A 1031 is done more by individuals, or their LLCs, than a syndication. This is just because it is easier with less people. A 1031 allows an investor to "defer" paying capital gains taxes on an investment property when it is sold as long as another "like-kind property" is purchased with the profit gained from the sale of the first property. If you do get into escrow to sell your property and want to 1031 into another property, try to find a replacement property ahead of time. Again, it's not easy to do in a syndication. Be sure to employ a professional and talk to your attorney about this. You don't want to notify your investors that you can 1031 when you actually cannot. Ultimately, you want to have a deal tied up in escrow and locked down right around the time the deal to sell closes, and you certainly want to have that done before the forty-five-day identification period is up. It is a balancing act because you don't want to have hard money at risk when your deal to sell is not finalized.

The sooner you start searching for the replacement property, the better off you are. If you wait until the eleventh hour and kind of identify some properties, you have more chance of not being able to meet the required deadlines. In these cases, you may end up identifying a property you don't actually have the ability to purchase. If you are short on time, you might feel the pressure to overpay compared to if you started thirty to forty-five days before the deal actually closed (which would give you a good sixty-to ninety-day window to try to find the replacement property).

If you are doing something a little bit more complicated like a tenant in common, you should employ a tax lawyer. Make sure you run through everything. Is there a rehab component to the new deal you are buying, or do you have some capex dollars that are going to generate boot? Boot is cash or other property added to an exchange to make the value of the traded goods equal. According to Investopedia, cash boot is allowed as part of a nonmonetary exchange under US Generally Accepted Accounting Principles.

Refinancing is a great tool to juice returns when there is a big value-add play. After you stabilize the property and have it seasoned per lender requirements, you can refinance and pay back a big chunk of the investor's money. Be aware of factoring in the cost of a refinance. However, market conditions can change on a dime, so you should be careful if you opt for a short-term loan, even when you plan to refinance. You can typically get a bridge loan with options up to five years. That is a decent amount of cushion to deal with curveballs. The beauty of a strong value-add play and refinance is if you can pay back your investors in full, they will have infinite returns going forward. Meaning, they just get cash flow and have no money invested in the deal anymore!

Some Asset Managers charge a fee to refinance and/or at disposition. Yes, there is extra work for the Asset Manager during refinance/disposition, but we feel it is part of your responsibility as an Asset Manager. It could be that, after a few tough ones, we may change our minds on this, but currently, we do not charge extra.

CONCLUSION

Congratulations, you've gone full cycle! Hopefully you profited greatly and in this case, with knowledge. There are many models out there and market conditions vary greatly, so you need to factor in your individual property and company situations when you consider refinancing or selling. There are a lot of big decisions we covered in this chapter. Do not feel you need to act in a silo. Reach out to your colleagues and seek opinions, but no one will know your business plan better than you—a Best in Class operator!

CHAPTER 17

TOOLS

Life is easier when you mind your own business.

—ANONYMOUS

This is the last chapter in your journey to becoming a Best in Class operator. Here, we won't deal with any step of your journey per se, but we'll provide you with a constant companion that can help transform your performance as an Asset Manager: tools.

Tools are what separate the amateurs from the pros. They can take you from being a "mom-and-pop" investor to a whole new level—that is, if you utilize these tools the way they are meant to be used. Many investors pay big bucks for these tools but never really use them, at least not at the level they are capable of. Having the right tools is one thing; using them to streamline your business and help you make better educated decisions is another.

Think of it this way. Imagine you're sitting in an airplane. It's going 550 miles per hour (mph) and has 200 miles of headwind. Guess what? The plane you are on has to work hard to keep that speed. But what if you turn the plane 180 degrees and go the other direction? Now you have a 200-mile tailwind and your plane can fly at 550 mph much more easily. This is what it is like when you start utilizing these tools—you put rocket fuel in your business and begin to grow exponentially.

Throughout this book, we've covered a number of tools that can help you at different stages of your real estate journey. Consider this chapter a compilation of what came before plus a few new tools that can transform your business. We use many of these tools ourselves and can promise they will make you not only a better Asset Manager, but also a better all-around real estate investor.

CUSTOMER RELATIONSHIP MANAGEMENT (CRM)

You might think you can get by without a CRM tool for a little while. Unfortunately, the more you put it off, the more you'll hurt yourself and your future. CRM tools can do a lot of things. Most importantly, they help you stay organized and ensure you store every contact so you get the value from your marketing and networking efforts. One day, you might find this database is worth more than the rest of your real estate business and assets put together.

Lead generation is expensive. It is even more expensive if you are throwing away 99 percent of your leads and deal opportunities. This is what you are doing if you don't have a CRM tool. All leads and contacts should go into your CRM tool. Then you can follow up, track your conversations, and close them. You can keep closing your leads as repeat customers. You can multiply them by extracting a lifetime of referrals from your leads. Each lead can provide many lifelong streams of income.

The best CRM tools will also offer a lot of automation so you can save enormous amounts of time. This will allow you to spend your hours on the highest-value tasks and keep your pipeline full at all times.

We will not go over each of these aspects in detail, but here is what you'll want to look for in a good CRM tool:

1. Integration
2. Ease of use
3. Speed of implementation
4. Support
5. Scale
6. Customization
7. Pricing

CRM options include HubSpot, Salesforce, Zoho, Propertyware, and Yardi.

INVESTOR PORTAL

Having an investor portal is no longer just a tool in your arsenal to attract and retain top investors; it's now a necessity. An investor portal is a gateway that allows your investors to view their investment portfolio. It also provides your investors with a more personalized user experience by giving them more control over their investments. This establishes a better relationship and more transparency between you and your investors. At the same time, an investor portal helps streamline your business and reduces the time you spend on things like calculating distributions and tracking performance. Here are some more benefits of having an investor portal:

- Visualize investments
- Manage portfolio
- Secure confidential information
- Download data
- Invest in new offerings
- Track performance
- Track equity raise

Investor portal options include SyndicationPro, Investor Deal Room, IMS, and Juniper Square.

MARKETING PLATFORM

Many professionals point to the death of email marketing

due to the growth of social media. However, according to a study done by McKinsey & Company, email marketing is up to forty times more effective than social media marketing as of the time this book was written. So for those that think email is dead, think again! To be successful with your email marketing, you need to have the right messaging and appeal to your audience, not the masses.

Having a marketing platform does not only mean email marketing; there are obviously many social media outlets that are just as important, and you should have a presence across these sites. But you do not own your contacts on social media. If those sites decide to change their algorithms or one day just cease to exist, what would you do? How would you get ahold of your audience at that point? This is why you need to have an email database that you own so you have control over your audience. This is where you want to build trust and establish relationships with your investors. Having a strong, consistent, and well-thought-out email marketing campaign and tool will allow you to develop the relationships you need to continue to grow your business.

Email marketing platform options include MailChimp, ActiveCampaign, Constant Contact, and AWeber.

TEAM COLLABORATION AND PROJECT MANAGEMENT

All Asset Managers, whether managing large or small properties and portfolios, will deal with many tasks, projects, plans, and people regularly. It takes teams of people working together to build a successful company. As you add more people to your team, not having a project management tool can make it very challenging to accomplish a task efficiently. The right tool can help run your business during the planning and execution of a project in an effective, predictable, and reliable way. Considering the advantages and service that project management tools offer, you can truly maximize the execution and efficiency of your teams. These tools can optimize the complete workflow, enhance productivity, and enable completion of projects in less time, which eventually leads to greater NOI. Here are some more benefits of having a project management tool:

1. Smooth collaboration
2. Easy and quick planning
3. Budget control
4. Easy resource allocation and management
5. Strong team workflow
6. Continuous project monitoring
7. Easy data sharing

Team collaboration and project management options

include Asana, ClickUp, Slack, Trello, Google Drive, Zoom, and CRM.

PROPERTY MANAGEMENT SOFTWARE

We discuss this in more detail in Chapter 7 (Managing the Manager), but property management software is definitely a tool you will want to access as an Asset Manager or owner operator. Whether you have your own property management company or you use a third-party company, the information is the same, and you will want to be able to see and use your data. This tool is where you will pull that data from and turn it into KPIs you will track and measure on a daily, weekly, monthly, and yearly basis. As an Asset Manager, this is where you will observe the pulse of your assets.

Property management software options include RealPage, Yardi, ResMan, and AppFolio.

MARKET ANALYSIS

Market analysis and compiling data are not just about the application of numbers. They are about living by what those numbers say and being courageous enough to walk away from perfect-looking deals when the data says they are not so great. Nowadays, it is so difficult to find great deals, and it's easy to convince yourself the one you are currently looking at is better than it really is. This is why listening to the data without emotion is so important, and you need the right tools to make that happen. Real estate is hyperlocal, so you want tools that not only tell you about the overview of a market but also can dial into the neighborhood where each property is located. Things like population growth, crime rates, jobs, rents, vacancy—these really matter in the neighborhood you are purchasing. Would it matter that you are in the best market in the country if you are purchasing a property in a neighborhood where all the metrics we just listed are trending in a negative direction and have been for the past several years? It would not! And trust us, no market has identical neighborhoods throughout—like we said, real estate is hyperlocal. Some of these tools can be very expensive, but there are also free tools out there that can provide you with a lot of this data.

Also be sure to leverage your network. People like brokers and property management companies have access to some of the best paid tools, and as you establish a relationship with them, they should have no problem sending you reports and information you may need.

Now, these reports are not just to be used before you purchase a property and to do due diligence on the neighborhood. As an Asset Manager, you want to consistently update yourself on the status of the neighborhoods of your current assets. As you track this information, you may come to the conclusion you need to change your business plan, whether it be due to bad or good news. If you don't know how the market is changing around you, it will be tough to make the right decisions for your properties. Staying up to date on this information through market analysis tools will make you a better Asset Manager and a better overall investor.

Market analysis tool options include Neighborhood Scout, RealPage, City-Data.com, DeptOfNumbers.com, Local Market Monitor, HousingAlerts, and CoStar.

BUSINESS INTELLIGENCE DASHBOARD

Business intelligence (BI) tools utilize a set of methodologies and technologies to prepare, present, and help analyze data, such as the KPIs we talk about in this book. Great BI tools help Asset Managers and owners ask and answer questions of their data. They show present and historical data within business contexts. Through this process, data is turned into actionable business information that allows you to make more effective, data-driven decisions.

Go to www.bestinclassbook.co to see a sample of our BI dashboard.

BI options include RealPage, Yardi, Tableau, and PowerBI.

TIME TRACKING

Time tracking is key to understanding how you spend your time, personally and in business. It is one of the keys to productivity, insight, and a healthy workflow. When you know which tasks take the most of your time, you can begin to reflect on whether that time is well spent. Time tracking allows you to make more intelligent decisions about how you price and run projects, schedule your team, and spend your day.

It is not only useful to track your time, but it is also useful to track your team's time. Being an Asset Manager or apartment owner is all about creating efficiencies and identifying bottlenecks. Time tracking makes this easier and allows teams to stay on task with ongoing projects. With time tracking, you can see where any potential hiccups are in the day-to-day workflow and use that insight to create strategies to help your team be more productive in the workplace.

If you are a real estate professional, these tools will also come in handy for tracking your hours for the IRS. As mentioned in our previous chapters, nothing matters until you actually need it. And you will need to show the IRS proof of the hours you are working and where they are being spent if you plan on qualifying for the real estate professional designation.

Time tracking options include Toggl, Hubstaff, SCREENish, and DeskTime.

VIRTUAL ASSISTANT

A virtual assistant can support your business by completing nonessential tasks, which will allow you to focus your time on the areas crucial to growing your business successfully. Training will be important when hiring a virtual assistant; you will need to set them up for success. We use a tool called Loom to record videos on all the tasks we want the virtual assistants to complete. This acts as a training tool and allows them to go back and review any time they have questions. We have also found that, by recording these videos, you tend to see holes in your own system; this then allows you to tighten it up prior to sending it off to the virtual assistant.

The way we determine which tasks to hand off is we apply an hourly rate to what we feel our time is worth (we broke this down in detail in Chapter 2). What you feel your time is worth will increase over the years, but if you are just starting out, maybe forty to fifty dollars an hour could be a good starting point for you. If there is any task you are currently doing that you could pay someone less than forty to fifty dollars an hour to do and that is not generating any revenue, you should pass it off to a virtual assistant. This is something that took us a long time to learn—looking back, we wish we started sooner. There is such a thing as time value of money, and the more time you are wasting on nonessential tasks, the slower your business and company will grow. Not to mention, the less time you will spend on the right things! Do not focus on what this will be costing you from a dollar standpoint. Focus on how much time it will free up for you and use that time for higher-dollar tasks (revenue-generating tasks). You will be glad you did!

Virtual assistant options include Upwork, Fiverr, MyOut-Desk, and Magic.

UNDERWRITING MODEL

Having a great underwriting tool can be the difference between finding opportunity and avoiding disaster. Many underwriting tools are built out of Excel and by someone else. How many times have you seen an Excel spreadsheet with an error, incorrect formula, or circular reference? One wrong formula can lead to inaccurate underwriting and change the returns of a deal substantially. So, the question is, do you trust your underwriting tool is free of errors? Does your model provide the flexibility you need to become an elite investor?

Much like many of the tools mentioned in this chapter that use data to allow you to make better decisions, an under-writing tool does the same. You want a tool that is going to provide you with data in the best format to allow you to make better decisions on your business plan and how a deal is underwritten. Online tools are improving rapidly. They can give you the advantage you need over your competitors as well as peace of mind that the formulas and calculations are correct. When seeking to improve performance, it is important to recognize underwriting is more than risk selection and pricing. You need a high-performance tool to get the best results when underwriting.

Underwriting model options include redIQ, Enodo, and Adventures in CRE.

INTEGRATION/AUTOMATION

This ties into many of the tools we mentioned earlier in this chapter. An integrated or automated business system is a mechanism for solving or executing issues or tasks that come up repeatedly and in a streamlined, effortless manner. Business systems can help solve inefficiencies for business owners in any industry, and real estate systems are no exception. Some qualities an integrated business system will typically possess include:

- Ability to address a specific problem or issue
- Automates business processes
- Solves inefficiencies
- Executes a process or routine

- Does not require intensive thought or effort once implemented

The advent of technology, including dynamic software and cloud-based solutions, has made it relatively easy for business owners to implement business systems and processes. However, it is impossible to do so without truly understanding the positive impact it can have on a business's bottom line. The following outlines several benefits of taking the time to implement real estate systems that work:

- Save time
- Reduce overhead costs
- Minimize errors
- Improve productivity
- Deliver consistent results
- Boost your bottom line
- Grow your business

First and foremost, real estate systems and processes can help business owners save time, so they can serve more investors and increase profits in less time. By implementing automated systems, manual labor hours can be cut down significantly. This directly translates into cutting down on the cost of labor, such as outsourced work or office assistants. The process of cutting down human labor hours through the integration of technology and taking away as many manual steps as possible also helps minimize human error. This prevents small issues from turning into bigger ones over time. Business owners can use this newfound free time to their greatest possible advantage.

A second area that cannot be ignored is the ability to deliver consistent results through the use of technology and automation tools. By designing and implementing effective systems, Asset Managers can ensure the delivery of efficient and repeatable results. Systems that produce reliable results ensure professionals can meet the needs and expectations of their clients in a consistent manner. This, in turn, improves the brand and increases the proportion of repeat investors. Finally, Asset Managers can devote their renewed availability of time and energy to activities that will help grow their assets.

CONCLUSION

There are certainly more tools you can add to your toolbox, and you will over time. The important thing is you consistently use these tools to improve your systems and business. The more you can focus on this, the quicker you will become an elite investor and Asset Manager.

Lastly, we wanted to leave you with one more goodie to help you along your journey. Technology becomes obsolete quickly, so we have created a section on our website, www. bestinclassbook.co, that updates the relevant software we mentioned every year. We hope you enjoy!

CHAPTER 18

CONCLUSION

An investment in knowledge pays the best interest.

—BENJAMIN FRANKLIN

Being a good Asset Manager takes a lot of hard work, but it is attainable for the diligent. Things change constantly, and business plans do not remain static. You must learn to pivot, put processes in place to deal with the unexpected, and know how to identify the fires and bottlenecks when they arise. Most importantly, you have to understand all aspects of the business as clearly as you can and make sure you have a good team to help you realize your vision.

We hope this book has impressed upon you the importance of starting *now*. Being proactive rather than reactive is what separates most of the good Asset Managers from the not-so-good ones. You can't wait for your property to be underperforming to start paying attention. You need to be on top of the property from day one—from the time you underwrite to the day you sell it. The upside you will receive from putting in the work is a huge return on your money—for both you and your investors (if you have any).

We hope you learned a lot from this book. We tried not to bore you with too many minute details but provide enough that this was worthwhile. We shared our experiences as well as the experiences of over 150 experts and friends we have interviewed over the years. If there's one thing we've seen throughout our careers, it's the value of community. Community is what made this book possible; it contains a diverse range of advice from like-minded people who've battled the same challenges as you and wanted you to learn from their mistakes. Community is why our field grows. We've seen the value of getting like-minded people on the same page—when it happens, great things can be accomplished. This is why we hope you'll continue to participate in our community once you close this book. Share your experiences on our multiple channels, including our Facebook Group: Asset Management Mastery. Contribute to further discussions on best practices in this field. This is how we can all take this field to greater heights.

We'll leave you with this thought: this is not where your journey ends but where it begins. This book will always be here for you to go through. Keep coming back if you need to review topics. We've designed this book to be your companion; use it as one. There are always new things to learn. Take advantage of our free online resources to expand your learning. Engage with our Facebook group to widen your knowledge and engage in conversation with other industry players. Connect, give back, share—we all grow from it.

And of course, we will always be here. If you feel like you need more guidance and want to continue your journey toward Asset Management Mastery with us, visit www.assetmanagementmastery.com to find out more about how we can help you. If you've enjoyed this book, leave a review on Amazon and Goodreads so other people can find it. And don't hesitate to connect with us on social media. You're part of the community now.

Kyle & Gary

ABOUT APT CAPITAL GROUP

We created APT Capital Group because there should be a more reliable way to accumulate wealth than the ever-fluctuating stock market and putting your hard-earned money into your 401(k). Ninety percent of the world's millionaires invest in real estate. Tax benefits, housing as a necessity, backed by a hard asset—these are some of the reasons why real estate, and specifically workforce housing, offers the best risk-adjusted returns out there.

APT Capital Group offers the chance for busy people to invest in real estate with experts who are aligned with their goals. Together, the managing members have over fifty years of management and operations experience. Our mission is to positively impact the lives of our investors and the communities in which we invest through the highest level of transparency and fiduciary responsibility. Our exceptional operations are our secret sauce. At APT Capital Group, we make it easy for investors to build wealth with people you can trust!

Made in the USA
Middletown, DE
13 July 2022

69150673R00149